BATTLE FOR THE HEART OF TEXAS

Battle for the Heart of Texas

Political Change in the Electorate

Mark Owens
Ken Wink
Kenneth Bryant Jr.

Foreword by
Robert T. Garrett

Library of Congress Cataloging-in-Publication Data

Names: Owens, Mark, 1984– author. | Wink, Kenneth A., 1962– author. | Bryant,
    Kenneth, Jr., 1985– author.
Title: Battle for the heart of Texas : political change in the electorate / Mark
    Owens, Kenneth A. Wink, and Kenneth Bryant Jr.
Description: Norman : University of Oklahoma Press, [2022] | Includes
    bibliographical references and index. | Summary: "Sifts a large cache of polling
    figures and qualitative data from surveys and focus groups to analyze Texas
    voters' nuanced opinions (about the 2020 Democratic primary candidates,
    about state and national government responses to the Covid-19 pandemic, and
    about issues such as immigration and gun policy), chart changes in Texas voting
    behavior over time, and describe emerging trends"—Provided by publisher.
Identifiers: LCCN 2022008539 | ISBN 978-0-8061-9074-7 (hardcover)
Subjects: LCSH: Voting—Texas. | Elections—Texas. | Political participation—
    Texas. | Political parties—Texas. | Texas—Politics and government—1951– |
    BISAC: HISTORY / United States / State & Local / Southwest (AZ, NM,
    OK, TX) | POLITICAL SCIENCE / Political Process / Political Parties
Classification: LCC JK4890 .O84 2022 | DDC 324.6/509764—dc23/
    eng/20220630
LC record available at https://lccn.loc.gov/2022008539

The paper in this book meets the guidelines for permanence and durability of
the Committee on Production Guidelines for Book Longevity of the Council on
Library Resources, Inc. ∞

CONTENTS

ACKNOWLEDGMENTS

A key to democratic representation is measuring, on a regular basis, the public's sentiment about their leaders and what preferences the public has. Texas is truly different from the rest of the nation, while the state finds itself at the forefront of national discussion about public policy. Our surveys of random registered voters in Texas contribute to a collective effort by researchers at the University of Houston and University of Texas that have surveyed Texas voters in years past.

This book was developed over four years. The first statewide survey we conducted in October 2018 offered a preview of the tightening U.S. Senate race between Senator Ted Cruz and U.S. Representative Beto O'Rourke. UT Tyler's role in Texas public opinion began in 2014 when Kenneth Wink and Barbara Hart led the East Texas Poll. Our ability to work with students to contact voters across the state from a lab on campus bolstered opportunities to look at public opinion in Texas in new ways. We benefitted from the dedication and special contributions of more than 150 students who have worked alongside us to interview voters. Their efforts were tremendous and continue to create new paths for future classes at UT Tyler. Our work is also made possible by the generosity and vision of investment administrators at UT Tyler. We are grateful for the support we received from Provost Amir Mirmiran, Dean Neil Gray, his predecessor Dean Martin Slann, Professor Marcus Stadelmann, and Professor Tom Guderjan. We are also indebted to Cheryl Cushatt and Ada Bravo, who support our work daily.

We must also thank our colleagues at the *Dallas Morning News*, who became true partners in our shared interest in understanding what Texans think about state issues. Mede Nix reinforced our mission to bring the public's voice to the forefront and offered amazing vision to keep survey topics at the appropriate level for the public to understand. Additionally, efforts by reporters in the Austin and Washington, D.C., bureaus revealed such interesting stories through follow-up interviews that gave context to the poll responses in support of outstanding articles by Bob Garrett, Todd Gillman, and Gromer Jeffers Jr. More stories by Allie Morris, Diane Solis, Sami Sparber, and Marin Wolf continued to connect findings from these polls to what was happening in Austin and communities across Texas. This book gives a broader perspective to these valuable descriptions of Texas during the campaign, the pandemic, and legislative session.

Finally, the arguments we share in this book are better and clearer because of the comments we received from Professor Kirby Goidel, Professor James Riddlesberger, Professor Keith Gaddie, and frequent conversations with Katie Owens about Texas politics.

A year into the coronavirus pandemic, and almost eight months after George Floyd's murder by a Minneapolis police officer, Texas Gov. Greg Abbott assured anxious conservatives that a steady stream of high-tech companies relocating from California would not alter the politics of the nation's biggest red state.

"The people who are coming from California are not going to turn Texas blue," Abbott said before a friendly audience at the Texas Public Policy Foundation, an Austin-based think tank that advocates free-market solutions.

Fortune 500 corporation executives who were moving their companies to Texas confided that a major reason they chose Texas was "lawlessness" in their home communities in liberal states, Abbott said. The two-term Republican governor used shorthand for the urban unrest that swept the nation in the aftermath of Floyd's suffocation death before onlookers on an American city street.

Over the previous four months, Abbott relentlessly had bashed the city of Austin for "defunding the police," a reference to a nearly 5 percent trim caused by cancelling three cadet classes, and Austin leaders' brief consideration of moving services such as forensics and the 9-1-1 call center out of police control.[1]

The issue helped Texas Republicans fend off Democrats' nationally publicized push to seize control of the Texas House. The 2020 election dashed Democrats' hopes of blocking or at least moderating plans for the Legislature the following year to ram through bills on "election security" and once-a-decade redistricting plans. With continued full control of both chambers, GOP lawmakers in 2021 produced favorable maps and new limits on mail ballots and drive through voting, all useful as they sought to extend an era of GOP dominance in Texas politics.

"Hold on, hold on, because stories are not good enough," Abbott said at the Texas Public Policy Foundation event. "This is a public policy organization. You expect data, and I have data."

Exit polls in 2018 that he paid for, the governor recounted, replicated a result that a CNN exit poll found in that year's close race between U.S. Sen. Ted Cruz and Democrat Beto O'Rourke: 57% of respondents who reported moving to Texas from California said they voted for Cruz. The first-term Republican senator and former presidential hopeful fared better among recent transplants from the Golden State than among native-born Texans.[2]

"That is the mentality of the people who are coming here," said Abbott, who noted there was a two-way flow of people. California is the "No. 1 destination of people leaving Texas," just as Texas is the most common target for relocating California residents. "We're involved in a big exchange program," he said. "We're taking their conservatives and we're sending them our liberals."[3]

In *Battle for for the Heart of Texas*, University of Texas at Tyler political scientists Mark Owens, Kenneth Bryant, and Kenneth Wink assay the two major political parties' relative strengths in the Lone Star State and wade into the controversy over whether it's becoming more competitive—always a delicate task, given the dangers of proclaiming a party realignment too soon.

Three big threats loom over continued Republican hegemony, they note: Minorities are growing as a share of state population. Young Texans are leaning more Democratic. And major cities not only are growing faster than the remainder of the state, they are becoming more diverse—and more Democratic. Perhaps as a byproduct, once-massive GOP support in the exurbs around those big Texas cities is waning, Owens, Bryant and Wink said, citing polling conducted by UT-Tyler and *The Dallas Morning News*.

Abbott's assertion that newcomers from other states wouldn't pry Texas away from the Republican Party, but would help keep the GOP in the driver's seat, evokes one of the markers for incipient party realignment laid out by Kevin Phillips in his prescient 1969 book, *The Emerging Republican Majority*. Time and growing disgruntlement—sometimes, the byproduct of success—can erode a governing majority's support, Phillips wrote. Obsolescence of a prevailing ideology also is a threat. So are the landmines of race and migration.[4]

Tacking against some unfavorable demographic and party-identification winds, Abbott and other Texas Republican leaders face several tasks. They must find ways to maintain their party's huge advantage among white voters, make inroads among racial and ethnic minorities (read that Hispanics and Asian Americans, for the most part), and limit the damage that populist conservatism (and even more so, Donald Trump-style nationalism) causes with younger voters and white women. The GOP also must hope that Texas' abundance of newcomers turns out to be mostly people who assimilate and embrace a state political culture that venerates business and rugged individualism. For the Texas GOP, new residents who question old customs are a threat.

O'Rourke's Senate candidacy had badly shaken GOP leaders and strategists in Austin. Victory margins of statewide Republicans such as Lt. Gov. Dan Patrick and Attorney General Ken Paxton fell to the low single digits. Abbott's January 2021 display of relief at the Texas Public Policy Foundation event also mirrored Texas Republicans' majority-maintenance tasks:

- Law and order is a wedge issue that has worked for Republicans since Richard Nixon, and it worked for Texas Republicans in 2020. It also, as Owens, Bryant, and Wink suggest, may help keep white women from bolting the GOP. At the Texas Public Policy Foundation event, Abbott said he worked hard to prevent a Democratic takeover of the Texas House, "to make sure that we do not allow cities to defund their police."

- Continued success by Texas at economic development buttresses arguments that the state's low tax, light regulation approach is working. As he ticked off a stream of relocations of corporate headquarters to Texas (Tesla, Oracle, Hewlett-Packard), Abbott said CEOs he's wooed are pleased that Texas has limited lawsuit awards in personal-injury cases and praise Texas' "superior workforce." One had recently quizzed him about how many years Texas can hold off having a state income tax, he recounted. "I can assure you we are not going to have an income tax in Texas far beyond your lifespan because [in 2019] we put it into the Texas Constitution that an income tax is not allowed in the state of Texas," Abbott said in reply.[5]

- Abbott spoke of the need to restore civics education in public school classrooms. It would be "focusing on Texas values, Texas exceptionalism, patriotism, the U.S. Constitution, the core values that have made Texas Texas—so that we inculcate our students from the very beginning with a lasting impression of exactly why Texas is great." On one level, Abbott's remarks can be read as an appeal for a generational replacement of the Texas GOP voting bloc. Yet they also were about wedge politics. In 2021, he and state lawmakers seized on civics education to firm up their support among whites of all ages. They passed two bills attacking "critical race theory" and a third touting a "Texas 1836 Project," a thinly veiled dig at *The New York Times'* "1619 Project," which sought to elevate the role of slavery and contributions of Black Americans in the national narrative.

- Finally, relocation of conservative voters from other states was on his mind. Clearly, were it an event with scale, such migration would help Texas Republicans cling to power. It's not clear, though, whether conservatives outnumber liberals relocating from other states. Still, the notion generates buzz. A failed California GOP congressional candidate, Paul Chabot, has moved to Collin County, north of Dallas. Four years after Chabot created Conservative Move, a realty company that helps Californians flee their state for redder territory, he ran for Texas state representative in 2022.[6]

Since Texas was admitted to the Union in 1845, it rarely has veered from conservative governance. Only major economic downturns—affecting farmers in the 1890s and the state's entire population during the Great Depression of the 1930s—produced startling exceptions. The administrations of Govs. James Stephen "Big Jim" Hogg (1891–1895) and James V. Allred (1935–1939) showed populist, anti-business tendencies. But they were deviations from the norm.

Since the 1950s, Texas has gone from two factions of the Democratic Party controlling the state to two factions of the Republican Party controlling the state.

For most of the first half of the twentieth century, and even a decade or so into the second half, Democrats ruled Texas. Supporters of former President Franklin D. Roosevelt's New Deal clashed with conservative dissenters. Race matters motivated the initial revolt by conservatives, though business regulation and the federal government's social programs also embittered some. Today, two wings of the Republican Party dominate Texas politics. There are pro-business conservatives. And there are populists who combine nativist appeals, libertarian leanings, and hardline stands on such culturally fraught issues as guns, gay rights, and abortion.

Republicans started making inroads with the election to the U.S. Senate of John Tower. In 1961, Tower became the first Republican from a former Confederate state to win a Senate seat by popular election. After the Vietnam war and the turbulence of the 1960s, many conservative Democrats in Texas followed former Gov. John Connally into the Republican Party. Connally, a protege of former President Lyndon B. Johnson during LBJ's congressional career, entered Nixon's cabinet as treasury secretary and was a frontrunner for the GOP presidential nomination that went to Ronald Reagan in 1980.

In the 1978 midterm elections, during Democrat Jimmy Carter's single term as president, Dallas oilfield-services magnate William P. Clements Jr. rocked Texas' political firmament by winning the governorship over then-state Attorney General John Hill, who had ousted a sitting Democrat in the primary. Clements was the first Republican governor of Texas since Reconstruction.

And Republican state Treasurer Kay Bailey Hutchison won a special election in 1993 for the U.S. Senate seat vacated by former President Bill Clinton's first treasury secretary, moderate-conservative Democrat Lloyd Bentsen. Hutchison's victory signaled the approaching end of Democratic potency in Texas. Once again, Republicans had won a statewide race by fanning popular discontent with a Democrat in the White House. And as Owens, Bryant, and Wink point out, two of their breakthrough wins in Texas—Tower's and Hutchison's—came in special elections, when Democratic voter turnout typically lags.

With the exception of a few down-ballot wins in 1994, Democrats' last marquee wins in important statewide races occurred when Ann Richards, a salty-tongued former state treasurer, narrowly captured the governorship in 1990 (though she couldn't win reelection); and when Bob Bullock, a wily, four-term former state comptroller, triumphed in races for lieutenant governor (an important post in Texas, unlike in some other states) in 1990 and 1994. Ironically, in 1973, Bullock had been one of few prominent Texas Democrats to chastise Connally for jumping ship to the GOP. A quarter-century later, though, he endorsed Richards' conqueror, Republican George W. Bush, for reelection as governor.

After the Richards-Bullock magic faded, things went mostly downhill for state Democrats until O'Rourke came within three percentage points of ousting Cruz in 2018. True, there were two Democrat-friendly election cycles late in George W. Bush's presidency, 2006 and 2008, after which the Democrats briefly threatened to regain control of the Texas House. A voter backlash against draconian budget cuts passed in 2003, when Republicans first gained full control of the Legislature, converged with growing voter disapproval of Bush's decision to invade Iraq and handling of the aftermath of Hurricane Katrina. Possible overreach by the state GOP on the legislative maps passed as part of former U.S. House Majority Leader Tom DeLay's mid-decade re-districting in 2003 combined with increasing populations of voters of color in the suburbs to create a seeming opening for state Democrats.

Barack Obama's historic election to the White House in 2008, though, and the backlash to his presidency and policies a year later, which helped to set in motion the tea party movement, reversed all of Texas Democrats' legislative gains. Indeed, in the 2010 general election, the GOP won 99 of the Texas House's 150 seats. After two Democrats defected, Republicans in the chamber enjoyed a supermajority in the chamber in the 2011 session—and retained 95 or more seats for the following three every-other-year legislative gatherings.

Then 2018 saw O'Rourke drive record turnout in a midterm election in Texas, yielding a harvest of congressional and legislative seats and state appeals court judgeships for the Democrats. In the Texas House, they were just nine seats shy of a majority entering the 2020 general election—the one in which the door closed again on further Democratic advances, thanks to fundraising and get-out-the-vote help from Abbott's organization and a solid statewide showing by U.S. Sen. John Cornyn. The three-term Cornyn beat Democratic newcomer and decorated Air Force veteran MJ Hegar by nearly 10 percentage points, even as Trump was besting Joe Biden in Texas by only 5.6 points. In the Legislature, as *Battle for Texas* went to press in 2022, Democrats suffered a party switch and a special election loss, and were down to 65 seats in the Texas House.

When I started covering the Legislature in 1979, as a still-green political reporter three years out of college, Democrats held 125 House seats. In the 31-member Texas Senate, they held 27. The biggest fight that session was over whether to help John Connally's looming presidential bid, by creating a presidential primary in March separate from one for state and local offices in July, thereby allowing conservative voters to help Connally while continuing to have a voice in the all-important Democratic primaries for non-federal office. An end-of-session walkout by a dozen liberal Democratic senators, known as the "Killer Bees," squelched the idea.

More than two decades later, after I'd covered legislatures in two other states and, for a brief time, Congress, Robert Mong, then editor in chief of *The Dallas Morning News*, helped ease my way back into covering Texas politics. Mong, who'd known me when I was the junior political writer at the now-defunct *Dallas Times Herald*, urged me to read John B. Judis and Ruy Teixeira's *The Emerging Democratic Majority*.

Consciously emulating Phillips' work from a generation earlier, Judis and Teixeira in 2002 proclaimed that a new Democratic coalition was forming that would dominate American politics. White working- and middle-class Democrats interested in economic security and turned off by Republicans' "laissez-faire dogma" would join forces with minorities, women ("especially single, working, and highly educated women") and professionals to support a "progressive centrism," they wrote. Demographic destiny was a key part of Judis and Teixeira's argument: By 2012, a swelling population of Hispanic, Asian, Black, and other minority voters would comprise one-quarter of the U.S. electorate, they wrote. Such minorities gave Democrat Al Gore at least 75 percent support in the 2000 presidential election. In Texas, Hispanics were 29 percent of the potential electorate, Judis and Teixeira said.[7]

Pointing to the "Dream Team" that Texas Democrats fielded in that year's midterm election, Mong told me things probably would start changing—and fast. But the Dream Team flopped. It consisted of a wealthy Hispanic businessman running for governor (Tony Sanchez), a pro-business, Black former mayor of Dallas for U.S. Senate (Ron Kirk) and a moderate white politician for lieutenant governor (John Sharp). Republicans won all of those 2002 races and by substantial margins—respectively, Rick Perry (who'd succeeded Bullock in the lieutenant governor's post and ascended to the governorship after Bush won the presidency in 2000); Cornyn; and David Dewhurst.

Perry went on to serve as governor for 14 years, followed by Abbott's gubernatorial run that lasted at least eight. Despite an upending in the past two decades of the Judis-Teixeira hypothesis, both nationally and in the state, *Battle for the Heart of Texas* authors Owens, Bryant, and Wink suggest Republicans' grip on the state may be loosening.

In the 2020 census, in raw numbers, Hispanics (11.4 million) almost caught up with non-Hispanic whites (11.6 million) in Texas. By 2050, Hispanics are projected to be the state's dominant racial-ethnic group, with more than 20 million of the state's expected total population of 47.4 million.[8] Getting Hispanics in the habit of voting, though, remains a challenge. And the fidelity of some to the Democratic Party is in question. Trump's surprisingly strong 2020 performance among Hispanics in South Texas spawned a flurry of efforts by the national and state GOP to try to woo Latinos by painting Democrats as socialists soft on crime and weak on border enforcement.

Urbanization, though, may cut against the GOP. With the exception of El Paso, West Texas has been a Republican stronghold for a generation. In 2020, however, just 13 percent of Texans lived in West Texas, defined as all counties west of those intersected by Interstate 35, according to state demographer Lloyd B. Potter. That's down from 17 percent in 2010.

Another vulnerability for Texas Republicans has been a perception they're playing to their most staunchly conservative "base" voters and not minding the store. Under Perry and Abbott, the Legislature responded to concerns about traffic congestion, reduced maintenance of roads in oil-drilling regions with "fracking" booms, rising local property taxes and the state's declining share of the tab for public schools by dedicating existing tax revenues to transportation and property tax relief, while at least temporarily boosting support for K-12 schools. In the state budget, that has squeezed health care and higher education programs. The February 2021 winter storm brought blackouts, misery, and deaths, after the state's main electric grid cratered. Neglect of such key infrastructure presented Democrats with another potential line of attack.

Texas Democrats, though, are plagued by their national party's growing identification with elites. It has hemorrhaged working-class whites to Trump's GOP. Growing polarization and nationalization of politics also may retard Democratic advances: In the 1960s and 1970s, a conservative Texas Democrat could edge over to the GOP relatively painlessly. The reverse — a flow of Republican voters away from their moorings — may be harder in an era of tribalistic politics. Fragmentation of traditional news media, the rise of Fox News and conservative talk radio, and the threat posed by social-media disinformation also complicate Texas politics, especially for Democrats.

As the state begins to approach the middle of the twenty-first century, it's also worth considering a question obliquely raised by Abbott's remarks, in his January 2021 live interview at the Texas Public Policy Foundation, about the state's "exchange program" with California: How enduring is Texas' political culture? Does the state change newcomers, or do they change it?

From the earliest settlement of Texas by whites in the early nineteenth century, its most powerful residents emulated the "haughty planter manner" of Old South aristocrats. They were intolerant of outside authority and saw government "as no more than a necessary evil," according to Southern Methodist University political scientist Cal Jillson.[9] The attitude persisted. In the twenty-first century, Abbott and fellow Republicans hope it flourishes to the state's bicentennial and beyond.

"They are fleeing California for a reason, they're fleeing New York for a reason," Abbott said of the corporate titans he spoke with about relocating their businesses. "They do not like the way that government is run in those states, and they like the way it's done here."

Robert T. Garrett
Austin Bureau Chief, *Dallas Morning News*
January 2022

CHAPTER I

Political Change in Texas

L ATE INTO THE EVENING of Tuesday, November 6, 2018, national television networks turned to Beto O'Rourke at a minor league ballpark in El Paso as he conceded defeat in Texas's race for the U.S. Senate. The improbable competitiveness of the race between Representative Beto O'Rourke and Senator Ted Cruz attracted national attention because it revealed how much of the presumed Republican advantage for any candidate had eroded just two years after Donald Trump won the state by a 9 percent margin.

Since 1998, Texas has been the most populous solid-Republican state in the country at the presidential and state levels. A surge of new voters during the 2018 midterm showed that a different style of politics could attract Texas voters to support a Democratic candidate. In his own words, Representative O'Rourke found enthusiasm for his candidacy in Republican strongholds like Midland, the center of West Texas's oil and gas economy. In March 2017, O'Rourke described the incipient momentum he recognized: "There's something that I feel everywhere, and not just in the usual places, that tells me this is possible."[1] The end result of this campaign was a new classification of Texas as a battleground state during midterm elections.

Would the 2018 election be a glimpse of the future? Could Texas Democrats compete against Texas Republicans in a presidential year? The results of the 2020 election showed the competitiveness of Texas's elections would be changed by the 2018 election. Beto O'Rourke continued to mobilize voters in Texas by running for president and subsequently creating "Powered by the People" to contact potential voters in Texas. These efforts contributed, in part, to the record turnout in the 2020 election that followed the registration of 2.2 million new voters. The shock of the 2018 election also spurred a counter mobilization effort by Texas Republicans who realized how influential urban areas were to political change in a high turnout election.

Texas politics reminds us that longstanding political change within states is frequently insulated from national forces. As the renewed partisan competition in Texas illustrates, political change is often discussed as a new alignment of voters who can reliably sustain a majority for multiple elections. Political scientists and historians have studied this question by tracking shifts in what issues define a political party's agenda, observing population movement into or out of a state, and the effect of laws designed to extend suffrage to new populations. John Gerring reminds us that political change rarely occurs universally at the national level.[2] Critical change is the result of the culmination of advancements by political groups over many years or a new response to shifting regional economies. Simply put, politics change. The composition of a constituency is dynamic.

Texas is an important bellwether for how we think of political change in America. The state has the second largest population in the Union. The Republican Party is interested in expanding because of migration to the state and the maturation of younger voters whom they hope will continue to vote for Republican presidential candidates. But recent anecdotal evidence indicates the Democratic Party may have momentum on its side to win elections again in the home state of Lyndon B. Johnson. Texas's large metropolitan areas are among the fastest growing in the country, and the electorate is becoming more racially diverse. Joe Biden's ability to get more votes than Donald Trump in Tarrant County, where Fort Worth and Arlington are, showed a Democratic nominee could win Texas's five most populous counties again, something that had not been done since 1964.

So, why has the increasing diversity of Texas's electorate not diminished the electoral strength of the Republican Party in Texas? Research by V. O. Key on the 1940s and Erickson, Wright, and McIver on the 1980s showed that a shift in Texas's political persuasion is not correlated as strongly with demographic change nationally.[3] Moreover, the history of Texas's partisanship cannot be explained by a party's attempt to gain power by appealing to the new voters. The consistency of a party's success in winning elections suggests leaders find ways to insulate themselves from the swings of economic fortune.

Texas faces a slow erosion of its current political era. Partisan candidates compete directly with one another to attract new votes from all age groups, ethnicities, and new residents of the state. The regional coordination of get-out-the-vote efforts by the Democratic and Republican parties does not mean that momentum will cancel the electoral fortunes of either party. With instances of direct conflict between the two parties at the county level, each election in Texas is a shifting jigsaw puzzle of 254 pieces to find a majority.

This book describes how parties have used cultural differences in Texas to build lasting political eras. Texas has experienced increasing urbanization and demographic change since the 1940s, and the state's political climate has changed in three different directions since that time. An understanding of these dynamics provides a guide for new cultures in Texas seeking to develop political power. The 2018 and 2020 elections showed voter participation is again on the rise. Increased voter participation, particularly in the metropolitan areas, presents a challenge to the strength of the Republican Party in Texas much like increasing voter participation in the 1940s and 1950s helped the Republican Party become competitive. The new level of political engagement in Texas can help us answer questions about the future of a younger and more diverse South and the nation.

Conclusions derived from our statewide surveys published with the *Dallas Morning News* provide insights regarding where Texas stands today. These insights become even more powerful when they are placed in the context of Texas's past voting history. Texas Republicans were able to break through the long-standing Democratic dominance (1848 to 1948) when candidates were able to win special elections and present themselves as government outsiders. After decades of competing with Democrats, Texas Republicans have controlled the government for a generation.

Texas and the Rest of the South

Texas elections have foreshadowed the rise of a newly dominant political party in the past. John Tower became the first successful Republican U.S. Senate candidate in any Southern state since Reconstruction. This moment of political change was possible because of a crowded special election to fill the seat vacated by Vice President Lyndon Johnson. Tower won the run-off that followed the special election by defeating conservative Democratic Senator William Blakley (D-TX) by less than 1 percent of the vote, after Blakley had captured the conservative Democratic vote to edge out U.S. Representative Jim Wright and Texas Attorney General Will Wilson, all of whom received more than 10 percent of the vote.[4] Texas Democrats, particularly liberals, were reluctant to support Blakley who had been appointed by Governor Allan Shivers, a Democrat who previously endorsed Dwight Eisenhower's reelection. Moreover, Blakley openly opposed the Kennedy-Johnson agenda as an appointed senator between Johnson's resignation from the Senate in January 1961 and the state's special election in May.

The longevity of Tower's twenty-four-year Senate career certified the viability of the Republican Party in Texas (1961 to 1985), even as it overlapped with the success of Democratic stalwarts Senator Ralph Yarborough and Senator Lloyd Bentsen. Tower was succeeded by Phil Gramm (R-TX), extending the time that Texas's pair of U.S. Senators were from different political parties until Senator Bentsen was appointed to be Treasury secretary for President Bill Clinton in 1993. In the special election to fill Bentsen's Senate seat, State Treasurer Kay Bailey Hutchison (R-TX) handily defeated Bob Krueger who had been a member of the Texas Railroad Commission until he was appointed to serve as a senator for six months by Governor Ann Richards (D-TX).

Senator Hutchison's election in 1993 made Texas the fifth Southern state to have two Republican senators since Reconstruction; following Mississippi, North Carolina, Tennessee, and Virginia. Since then, Texas and Mississippi are the only two of those states that have continued to elect the Republican candidate for Senate in each election. The stories of how Tower and Hutchison were both elected show the unique circumstances that can be attributed to the growth and consistency of the Republican Party in the South.[5] The advantage of focusing the attention of disaffected voters in the election to participate in those low turnout elections has not been forgotten by the Republican leaders who have followed and avoided the need for statewide special elections.

History of Partisan Change in Texas

The results of presidential elections in Texas have often matched the other ten states of the former Confederacy, but occasionally Texas's independence shines forth and portends the beginnings of changes in regional trends. The voting history of Texas in presidential elections can be structured into three distinct periods since the United States annexed Texas in 1845. Texas was a reliable Democratic state from 1848 to 1948. Then the Republican Party began to win some elections in Texas between 1952 and 1976. Texas became a solid Republican state after the 1980 presidential election. We introduce these three periods of Texas's electoral history by tracking support for national party nominees in presidential elections. Each exhibits the fingerprints of how race, urbanization, a growing economy, and the fracturing of factions that created a majority coalition in the dominant party changed the political landscape of the state.

Blue State: Annexation to World War II, 1848 to 1948

The first major shift in the mass partisanship of Texas was a long-term erosion of the Democratic coalition. Powerful Texas Democrats in Washington could communicate the goals of the Conservative Coalition that maintained a national majority, which included Democrats in urban areas of the Northeastern states and White conservative Democrats in the South. The end of Texas's White primary for the Democratic nomination significantly reduced the early political power of White conservative Democrats. This significant change occurred at the same time intraparty divisions hardened as the New Deal grew and Texas became less agrarian. This fracturing of White conservative Democrats over which national party nominee they would support for president created a new, politically competitive state.

Texas's initial influence on national politics emerged from the state's resources and its expansion of Southern votes. Historian Joel Silbey pointed to the annexation of Texas in 1845 as the action that emboldened the Southern states to believe they had the economic strength to challenge the power of the Northern states.[6] Prior to the Civil War, Texas remained politically distinct from the rest of the South by voting for Democratic candidates. Then, when the 1860 presidential election was contested by four viable candidates, Texas's electors voted for John Breckinridge (Constitutional Union Party) of Tennessee.

Texas remained politically different from other Southern states as it rejoined the Union during Reconstruction. Between 1872 and 1948, Texas split from the Solid South during three key elections. In 1872, the states of Georgia, Tennessee, and Texas voted for Horace Greeley (Liberal Republican) in opposition to President Ulysses S. Grant. Then in 1928, Texas was the only Southern state to vote for Herbert Hoover (R) over Al Smith (D-NY). Also, in 1948 Texas did not support the candidacy of Dixiecrat Strom Thurmond (SC), instead voting for President Harry Truman (D).[7]

The long period of Democratic dominance in Texas's elections became more tense during and after the administration of Franklin D. Roosevelt (FDR). Despite the central role that Speaker Sam Rayburn (D-TX) and many members of the Texas Congressional delegation played in passing new laws during the Roosevelt administration, a growing cadre of Texans at home actively opposed FDR. A faction known as the Texas Regulars formed within the Texas Democratic Party. The national programs established to respond to the Great Depression and improve economic conditions in the 1930s coincided with the discovery of the East Texas oilfield in Overton, Texas, with Daisey #3. Prospectors, rough necks, and wildcatters were finding wealth in their own communities. The emergence of the independent oil baron substantially changed politics, because new billionaires—Roy Cullen, H. L. Hunt, Clint Murchison, and Sid Richardson—used their wealth to influence elections.[8] Political propaganda diminished Franklin Roosevelt's popularity in Texas and framed First Lady Eleanor Roosevelt as a socialist. The common themes were opposition to communism and the national Democratic Party and support for helping individuals succeed.

Political Change Follows the End of the White Primary

The all-White primary was the most prevalent Jim Crow policy in Texas's elections and was used statewide for the first time in the 1924 election, once a state law excluded non-White citizens from the Democratic primary. Previously, the decision to exclude Texas voters from primary elections because of race was made at the county level as early as 1903. East Texas counties, which rest at the end of the South's Black Belt,[9] used primary elections to exclude voters based on race and by doing so disenfranchised African Americans that made up most of the population in the region.

As the fracturing of the Democratic coalition along ideological lines between those loyal to Roosevelt and the Texas Regulars continued, the use of the White primary to limit candidates who could receive the Democratic nomination abruptly ended. The all-White Democratic primary fell when the Supreme Court ruled it was unconstitutional in *Smith v. Allwright* (1944). The case was the court's fourth decision about different adaptations the Texas Democratic Party tried to use to prohibit Blacks and Tejanos from voting to pick leaders of the state. In 1944, Houston dentist Lonnie Smith claimed his right to vote could not be protected if African Americans were excluded from primaries because primaries are an integral part of the electoral process. Smith's lawsuit was supported financially by the National Association for the

Advancement of Colored People (NAACP) to overturn *Grovey v. Townsend* (1935), which exempted the Democratic Party from the prior precedent involving the right of a party to determine the qualifications of its own membership.

The continued involvement of the Texas NAACP in challenging the inconsistency of Texas's election rules for two decades represents the strong foundation of civic engagement of racial minorities in Texas. During this time most Black Texans were registered as Republicans. As in most of the South, part of this Republican identity can be attributed to an affinity to the party of Lincoln, but part of it also was due to the structural exclusion of Blacks from the Democratic Party. The absence of literacy tests in Texas meant that the removal of the White primary in Texas created ways for African American and Tejano voters in Texas to participate in elections that were crucial to selecting who would represent them. The Texas State Historical Association estimates the number of African American residents registered to vote increased by seventy thousand between 1940 and 1948. That number reflects the optimism cultivated by NAACP grassroots activity and by more favorable voting conditions.[10] The result for the Democratic Party was that without the institutional tools to guarantee who would win an election, the state party became more dependent on candidates to win elections on their own. But the long-term effects for African American voters were profound; by the year 2000, between 65 to 70 percent of age-eligible, non-Hispanic Blacks were registered to vote, only roughly 4 percent below the registration rates for non-Hispanic Whites.[11]

Swing State and Individualism: 1952 to 1976

Texas supported Denison, Texas native General Dwight Eisenhower for president over Adlai Stevenson (D-IL) in 1952 and 1956. Eisenhower broke through the solid Democratic South in Florida, Tennessee, and Virginia, thereby advancing the party's status within Southern states and Texas.[12] Before the Voting Rights Act of 1965, the bleak electoral opportunities for non-native son Republican candidates in Texas depended on support from Black voters and the growing urban areas, just like Northern states.

After the 1950 Census, Texas remained the sixth most populous state in the Union. In a decade where the South had grown faster than the rest of the nation, Texas held ten more Electoral College votes than Virginia—the next largest state population in the South.[13] Politics within the state was also changing with increasing urbanization, but the power of incumbency and the magnanimous reputations of Speaker Sam Rayburn and Majority Leader Lyndon B. Johnson were reminders of how important individual Texans were for preserving the Democratic Party's majority and the shrinking Conservative Coalition. In fact, Democratic nominees for president won Texas in all three of the presidential elections in the 1960s. The nuance behind each election suggests Texas voters were less responsive to the Southern strategy of Republican candidates than voters in other Southern states. Texans supported Senator John F. Kennedy (D-MA) in 1960, who ran with the state's own Senator Lyndon B. Johnson (D-TX). Texas celebrated another four years for President Lyndon Johnson by voting to defeat Senator Barry Goldwater (R-AZ), who campaigned heavily in the South in 1964.

The 1968 election showed the introduction of an extreme alternative could disrupt the electorate in Texas. Governor George Wallace (I-AL) attracted 19 percent of the Texas vote in the 1968 election as a third-party candidate, which showed the break-up of the Conservative Coalition. Johnson's vice president, Hubert Humphrey (D-MN) edged out former Vice President Richard Nixon (R-CA) by 1 percent of the vote in Texas, but all the Electoral College votes were awarded to the candidate who only received 41 percent of the vote. Four years later in his run for reelection, President Nixon carried Texas with 66 percent of the vote in his landslide reelection with the support of many of the voters who previously voted for Wallace.

The roots of Republican affiliations in Texas grew slowly during this time (1952–1972), mostly in the suburban areas. Nixon's 1972 landslide campaign in Texas only yielded a one-seat gain for Texas Republicans in the U.S. House, and only four of Texas's twenty-four U.S. Representatives were Republican after Texas added a new congressional district through the 1972 U.S. Census Bureau's reapportionment. These small gains were not insignificant, given that in 1952, Democrats had held all of Texas's twenty-two congressional districts. The twenty years between 1952 and 1972 also saw twenty new Republican members of the Texas State House, of which there were none after the 1952 election.

Texas remained a battleground state with twenty-six Electoral College votes in 1976 by voting for Governor Jimmy Carter (D-GA) over President Gerald Ford (R-MI).[14] After the unique election of 1976, Texas elected Bill Clements as the first Republican governor of Texas since Reconstruction. Those elections marked the end of an era when election outcomes at the presidential level varied election to election. With a Republican senator, Republican governor, and a growing number of elected representatives, the Texas

Republican Party was able to establish itself as a viable alternative at every level of government.[15]

In this era that followed the end of the Texas White primary, state elections remained free from federal oversight that covered other states in the South with the Voting Rights Act of 1965.[16] The voter protections of the Voting Rights Act were extended to Texas after the 1980 Census through the inclusion of Section 203 in the 1975 reauthorization of the Voting Rights Act. The census calculated the number of the voting-age population of American Indian, Asian American, Alaskan Native, and Spanish-heritage communities. Identifying the number of the population set the requirement for reducing barriers for citizens of language minorities based on the four criteria of Section 203's formula. The result of the census determined Texas had to comply with the federal Voting Rights Act because the number of voting-age citizens with Spanish heritage was greater than ten thousand and the rate of voting-age citizens with an education of less than the fifth grade was higher than the national average.[17] As a result, the state of Texas and many counties in west and south Texas were required to provide ballots in Spanish and seek federal approval for any future change to their elections. The attention to Hispanic heritage in the 1980 Census provided more precise information on how the state's population had changed as migration patterns changed during the fourteen years that followed the removal of immigration quotas by the Immigration and Nationality Act of 1965. Prior to that period only 30 percent of new residents to the United States from other countries came from non-European countries. After this point, migration from Latin America could expand, and the population of foreign-born individuals in Texas who could pursue citizenship increased dramatically.

The removal of a major barrier to voting for Tejano and Black voters prompted new coalitions in the electorate that varied election by election in response to the candidates more than their party. While the population of Texas began to have a larger share of Latinos and urban dwellers, the election outcomes were often associated with the level of agreement among White voters. At the same time, by 1976, Texas liberals had won control of the Democratic Party apparatus from the conservatives who had dominated the party for decades.[18] The modern Texas that reflects the political demands of White, Black, and Latino voters did not emerge until the next era when the Republican Party held equal or greater political power than the Democratic Party in Texas.

Rising Red Texas: 1980 to 2020

A forty-year streak of Republican nominees for president winning the state of Texas continued with the 2020 election. A Republican has won the state of Texas in eleven consecutive elections, two shy of the Democratic dominance in consecutive elections from 1876 to 1924. A reflection on how much longer Texas will remain a solid-Republican state requires a comparison of what has transpired since 1980.

Mass public opinion in Texas was more sensitive to the partisan coalitions in the state than the rest of the South between 1976 and 1988. Erikson, Wright, and McIver (1993) used multiple CBS News/*New York Times* surveys to measure public opinion during the period, and more Texans identified with the Republicans during national-level elections. As this shift occurred, Texans continued to identify heavily as conservative rather than as moderate or liberal, even exceeding the conservatism of most other Southern states. In fact, the mean percentage of voters in all polls who identified as conservatives versus those who identified as liberals was higher in Texas (+23.2%) than in any other Southern state except Mississippi (+25.4%). Erikson, Wright, and McIver also found Texas to be "an example of a relatively conservative and relatively polarized party system" (1993, 114). Texas showed signs of more mass ideological polarization than in any other Southern state. Republicans overwhelmingly identified as conservative rather than liberal (43.6% difference) while far fewer Democrats identified as conservative rather than liberal (+9.8%).[19]

The alignment of Texas conservatives who supported Republican candidates for president in Texas in the 1980s did not appear to be influenced by the demographics of the state. Texas was one of the most conservative electorates in the country, and it has a smaller White population. If the correlation between demographics and ideology operated in Texas as it did in most of the rest of the United States, Texas should have been moderate in ideology and balanced in terms of partisanship.

Ronald Reagan, in 1980, was successful in recruiting Democrats to his cause. His running mate George H. W. Bush provided an explicit appeal to many of these Democrats who "converted" to the Republican Party. The 1980s also brought young eligible voters who identified as Republicans in much larger numbers, setting the foundation for generational change when compared to previous cohorts of young adults. The rise of the religious right as a national political force in the 1980s deeply affected the Texas electorate. The movement channeled the conservative social beliefs of fundamentalist Protestants to political activity in favor of the Republicans.[20] The Republican Party's courtship of the evangelical Protestant church leadership began to shift the partisan balance in some states, including Texas.[21]

The expansive urbanization of Texas between the 1950s and 1980s transformed the state and reduced the proportion of rural White conservative voters who supported the conservative Democrats. The pro-business attitudes and actions of Reagan-style Republicans were able to bring together a unique coalition of some urban areas and the conservative ideologies of those in small towns. The blend was a preference for "[l]ow taxes and high tech, few barriers to opportunity but a less elaborate safety net, moving away from reliance on agriculture and oil, bypassing the era of big factories and big unions of the Great Lakes and eschewing the liberal cultural values of the two coasts."[22] Texans rode economic development into a state of partisan balance that resembled the rest of the United States when many other Southern states were entrenched in older patterns.

The Reagan-Bush victory in Texas in 1984 was the highest vote share of Texas voters in a presidential election—64 percent—at that time. Texas was pivotal in keeping a Republican in the White House by electing George H. W. Bush in 1988. Texas continued to support the Republican nominees in 1992 and 1996. Then in 2000, Governor George W. Bush (R-TX) received the highest vote share, 59 percent, for a Republican seeking a first term in office. Four years later, 61 percent of Texans voted to keep George W. Bush in the White House. The margin of victory in Texas for Republican nominees John McCain (R-AZ) and Mitt Romney (R-MA) were less than George W. Bush, but both were still more than 10 percent. Donald Trump's victory in 2016 by more than 9 percent in Texas fit with trends of large victories for a Republican nominee in Texas throughout the twenty-first century.

Despite Republican dominance in presidential elections after 1976, the 1990s were the pivotal decade of change in Texas politics. Until that time, conservative Democratic candidates benefited by the fact that they would win support from conservative and moderate Anglo voters in the Democratic primary, allowing them to win against more progressive Democratic candidates. In fact, in congressional races as late as 1992, it was not unusual for Democratic primary winners to win with a biethnic or even a triethnic coalition.[23] Then in the general election, the Democratic nominee would win support from more liberal Democrats of all races and enough conservative Anglo voters to defeat the Republican opponent. But as Texas politics became as polarized as national politics, with White voters increasingly opting to support the more economically and socially conservative Republican candidates in highly visible elections, Republicans became the new dominant party in the state from 1990 to 2000. Anglo votes for all Democratic candidates for statewide election—regardless of the race or ethnicity of those candidates—declined from typically 45 to 50 percent in the early 1990s, to 30 to 35 percent in the late 1990s, to 20 to 30 percent after the year 2000.[24] Republicans have won every U.S. Senate race since 1990, every governor's race since 1994, at least six of the nine constitutionally elected executive branch offices since 1994, and they finally took control of the state senate for the first time since Reconstruction in 1996.[25]

Democrats have attempted in vain to roll back this partisan trend toward the Republicans. For example, going into the 2002 elections, Texas Democrats were in search of a new identity. They retained control of the state House of Representatives but were only one election removed from the clean sweep of all statewide offices by Republicans in 1998. Moreover, Governor George W. Bush, who had defeated Governor Ann Richards, was no longer on the ballot. To engage new voters, the Democratic Party recruited candidates to fill the "Dream Ticket." Democrats nominated former Dallas Mayor Ron Kirk, an African American, to run in the open Senate seat against then Attorney General John Cornyn. Tony Sanchez, a Latino banker, won a divisive primary to challenge Rick Perry, who was elevated to governor when President George W. Bush resigned the position. The third member was former comptroller John Sharp, who had previously run for lieutenant governor in 1998 and lost to Rick Perry by 2 percent. The ticket was designed to engage Texas's diverse electorate on the assumption that descriptive representation, specifically among Latinos, would increase turnout among the largest minority population.[26] This experiment by Texas Democrats was not enough to overcome the Republican advantage in the state. All three Democratic candidates lost their elections, and down ballot Republicans were able to win enough seats to gain a majority in the Texas House, giving Republicans unified control of the Texas government for the first time since Reconstruction. Texas Republicans used their new political power to redraw the political boundaries of legislative districts at the federal and state level, which set the table for additional Republican gains in the Texas delegation to the U.S. Congress in 2004.

The Republican Party of Texas's cultural appeal to voters can be traced to how it responded to the 1992 presidential election. The Texas billionaire Ross Perot appealed to 22 percent of Texas's voters with populist rhetoric by saying the government needs to work for the people. After Perot drew voters away from Bush and Clinton, Texas Republicans like George W. Bush began advocating for new reforms the public easily understood like balanced budgets and less government regulation.

Texas Democrats have remained committed to encouraging racial and ethnic diversity in the state since the 2002 election. Greater attention has also been placed on cultivating a majority in the electorate by attracting women to their coalition. Texas Democratic Party rules require at least one of the two delegates from every county be a female on the Texas State Democratic Executive Committee. The decades of commitment to inclusion suggests that the Texas Democrats are making attempts to change the political culture of Texas in ways that will overcome the distinct electoral success Texas Republicans have continued to achieve as the state's diversity increases.

The Fracturing of Texas's Unique Political Culture

The 2020 election generated a new belief that the work Texas Democrats invested into shaping their image to represent a visible contrast to Texas Republicans might have reached a critical share of the masses. The gradual accumulation of electoral defeats of Texas Democrats in the 1980s and 1990s created an era where the party no longer had experienced leaders in office like John Sharp, who ran in 1998. The bet for Texas Democrats that the era of Republican dominance would be ending was the question of whether voters would reject Republican candidates who favored populism over pragmatism.

Texas Republicans faced a difficult political landscape in the 2020 election, which led news organizations like CNN to classify Texas as a battleground state.[27] The designation reflected three trends that showed Texas's electorate was changing. The sitting president, Donald Trump, was only popular with 45 percent of Texas voters. In the previous election, 2018, Senator Ted Cruz received 50.9 percent of the vote, the lowest vote share by a Republican in decades. Moreover, the Republican Party was attracting a smaller percentage of the vote in each of the three previous elections. Did this mark a change in Texas's political culture, at the same time the share of new voters in Texas were not majority White?

The strength of the Republican Party's inroads with independent voters succeeded again in 2020, as President Donald Trump won Texas with 5.6 percent more of the vote than Joe Biden. In that same election year, Senator John Cornyn won reelection with 10 percent more of the vote than M J Hegar. A comparison of the two vote shares points to the return of different levels of political safety for a party in presidential and subnational elections. Is that difference reflective of the contrasting political styles of both candidates that would favor candidates like Senator Cornyn who use less inflammatory language? Perhaps, but the overall share of the vote that Republicans are winning has been decreasing with Senator Cornyn receiving 54 percent in 2020, President Trump receiving 52 percent in 2020, and Senator Ted Cruz receiving 51 percent of Texas's votes in 2018 after a decade of much larger Republican vote shares in previous elections. If the trend continues there will be fewer voters willing to support some Republicans over others.

To this point, Republicans have maintained their majority with their emphasis on promoting economic growth and replacing votes lost in urban areas with votes from elsewhere in the state. Challenges for the party emerge when blocks of voters and regions of the state do not feel their economy is improving and when voters believe efforts by lawmakers to meet the demands of cultural conservatives distract from the goal of economic growth. For an era of political change that was initiated by Republicans winning most of the votes in Texas's largest counties, the political map of Texas looks much different today. Election returns from Bexar County, the second most populated county in Texas, show last time a Republican nominee for president won a majority of the votes in Bexar County was George W. Bush in 2004. In the years since, the county that is home to San Antonio has continued to grow in its total population and number of Latino residents. Also, the *Dallas Morning News's* endorsement of Hillary Clinton in 2016 marked the first time its editorial board endorsed a Democratic candidate since 1940.[28] The two examples signal that demographic change in Texas is accelerating and this is occurring at the same time as political elites are beginning to shift in their political preferences.

In this book we offer a view of where Texas stands in this time of political transition by focusing on mass public opinion. We explain what is occurring in Texas by documenting events that have already occurred, the new trends uncovered from interviews with voters, and by applying logic from research about public opinion and state politics. The approaches are combined to provide a comprehensive discussion about why the continued urbanization and demographic changes have developed a new political culture that has the potential to challenge Texas's political tradition. The book also explores if there are characteristics of political candidates that are attracting different factions of voters to generate the majority of votes required to win.

Theories of Political Change

The three eras of continuity in Texas's elections are connected to events that accelerated the change at the end of the time period. Like other studies of voting behavior, these changes reinforce the importance of institutional change and cultural change. For the first time, Texas approaches a moment when demographic change and generational replacement over the past forty years present new questions.

Texas is poised for a change, but it may still be characterized mostly as a hybrid individualistic-traditionalistic state. The typology of individualistic, moralistic, and traditionalistic states was described by Daniel Elazar in 1984 to describe the diversity of political subcultures in American federalism. The *individualistic subculture* reflects states like Texas that promote policies that are pro-business and anti-government (or at least "smaller" government) to incentivize the drive of the individual to prosper. The *traditionalistic subculture* emphasizes the primary role of government to maintain law and order, particularly in ways that support the status quo.[29] Because Texas's elected leaders are most often social elites and the conservative Democrats and Republicans who have led the state emphasize both business and order, the state does not easily fit into one category. Other examples of public life in Texas do not reflect a moralistic subculture where government service is admired to contribute to the public's interest and minority viewpoints are routinely considered.[30]

We contend that Texas's political culture has changed in important ways over the last few decades and eroded the remaining influence of the traditionalistic political culture Texas inherited. These changes are different from the class-based change in Texas V. O. Key and Chandler Davidson predicted would occur decades ago.[31] Elazar's theory of political cultures rested in the dominant ancestry of settlers to a region, but today Texas's population has been reshaped by the migration of people who have chosen to live there. First, immigration from Mexico with the subsequent increase in Latino voters is affecting the party system in Texas. Latino voters do not represent a monolithic voting bloc, even though they tend to favor Democrats over Republicans, if slightly. The Latino vote is the great unknown in any election, both in terms of party support and voter turnout. On the face of it, Latinos may reshape the party system in the state, likely making the partisan balance more even or balanced over time. Since neither party can afford to take the Latino vote for granted, in almost no place in Texas can a candidate for statewide office and many—if not most—candidates for state legislative office win without a biethnic (or triethnic) coalition of voter support. This is particularly true for Democrats in the state legislature and in congressional primaries and general elections, where triethnic coalitions are not uncommon but where the winner is often dependent on the specific type of coalition (triethnic or biethnic) that dominates in the district and the ethnicity of the Democratic candidate(s).[32] Of course, legislative redistricting (often accompanied by partisan gerrymandering) has had a substantial impact on partisan (and ethnic) representation in Texas congressional and state house delegations much as it has in the rest of the South since majority-minority districts began to be drawn in earnest in the 1990s in compliance with the Voting Rights Act of 1965.[33]

Second, in-migration from other states has and will continue to have a profound impact on Texas politics. During the latter half of the twentieth century, Americans from neighboring states and from outside the South poured into Texas seeking economic opportunity. Many of these migrants were educated and upwardly mobile, and those coming from outside the South tended to be more Republican than native Texans. Migration to Texas from neighboring states and from other states continues to this day, mostly bolstering the large and growing urban centers in the state.[34] While the suburbs of major metropolitan areas in Texas were Republican strongholds for the last fifty years, these suburbs are becoming more diverse and less Republican as the suburbs themselves become large cities with urban problems. Indeed, six of the top one hundred standard metropolitan statistical areas (SMSAs) of the United States, ranked by population, are in Texas. The smallest of these six is El Paso, with a population of more than eight hundred thousand that has likely grown in population by about 5 percent since 2010. The other five SMSAs have grown by 12 to 30 percent in the last decade, among the highest growth rates of SMSAs in the country. In fact, it is estimated that Dallas and Houston have held their respective rankings as the fourth and fifth largest SMSAs in the nation, and each is poised to pass Chicago in population in twenty years.[35] This urbanization has been fueled by many trends, but recent in-migration of highly educated and upwardly mobile workers from the coasts and from the Midwest certainly point to a likely change in partisan voting behavior in the suburban areas. Even native Texan migration from the more rural and conservative areas of the state is not likely to overcome the demographic changes of in-migration and migration from Mexico, and the tendency of people in large and quickly growing suburbs to turn to government for answers to problems related to infrastructure, education, health, and welfare. We will document the change in voting patterns in these suburban areas later in the book.

Third, generational replacement can result in political changes at times. One aspect of the change in party dominance in the South was the passing of older, conservative Democrats who had grown up in hardscrabble, rural areas in the nineteenth and early twentieth centuries and the birth of their grandchildren in the 1940s, 1950s, and 1960s. The grandchildren tended to grow up in larger towns and cities and in relative affluence when compared to previous generations. The early baby boomers came of age in the 1960s when traditional social mores were under assault, and many more of them attended college and became career professionals. Some opted to become Republicans, while others became more liberal Democrats. The later baby boomers born in the 1960s came of age in the 1970s and 1980s and experienced the backlash against the perceived excesses of the 1960s and hit college during the Reagan Revolution. These later baby boomers were often politically conservative, but equated conservatism with the Republican Party, not the Democratic Party.[36] The three authors of this book, all college professors, wonder if we are not seeing a similar sort of generational replacement today that may challenge the political culture in the state and may also challenge the dominance of the Republican Party in Texas politics. While it is too early to say that eighteen to thirty-year-olds will clearly break with the politics of their grandparents, we will investigate the possibility that the youngest voter cohort is significantly more liberal in their political opinions and voting behavior than the oldest voter cohort in our studies. If so, we will speculate on what that could mean for Texas politics in the not-too-distant future.

2018–2020 Creates Another Staggered Realignment for the New South

Movements like Me Too and Black Lives Matter reflect a nationalized political atmosphere that expanded how many people believe that they can make a difference in their community if they collectively support change. The rallies symbolized the solidarity of communities across the nation in order to signal attention on elected officials in Texas. Democratic lawmakers embraced the political movements, while Texas Republicans either avoided the issue or labeled the movements as outcomes of a larger socialist and leftist revolution. Those behavioral differences set a distinct contrast of the leadership styles that elected representatives are using to reinforce the political culture they would like Texas to have.

The logic from prior hypotheses of political change and the increasing political engagement of those who feel un-represented in Texas sets the stage for a realignment of Texas's political climate. The direction of that political change depends on the leverage that each region of the state has on an election outcome. As a result of the decision by both parties to protect their gains in regions of success, any future change is likely to occur across an extended period. The outcome of a prolonged shift is that Texas could develop a new political culture as it grapples with the interaction of its traditionalistic and individualistic past and the understanding by a large share of voters that they could have the power to change the system.

How the Voters See the State

The use of populist appeals by candidates seeking office in Texas since 2010 is an interesting phenomenon because it is occurring in the absence of a movement toward socialism. The review of Texas's political history in this chapter shows that populism has been strategically employed by candidates to attract votes from disaffected voters who can be persuaded by plans to put Texas before the national needs (statism).

The extensive questionnaires and frequent surveys of Texas voters on which we base our insights provide depth to examine how the electorate is shaping the actions of lawmakers. The foundation of this work extends from 23,750 interview responses that can give accurate assessments of the electorate at specific timepoints and tell a broader story of where Texas has been and what happens after the 2020 election. The ability to make both types of comparisons is essential to understand why support for statewide Republican candidates has deviated from past levels for some and a few Republicans candidates have kept pace with past trends.

The following chapters reveal that new voters and independent voters are shifting their political support away from the persistence of populism within the Republican Party of Texas. The lessons are important for the future of American politics, which is an aggregation of the timing and magnitude of political change at the state level. Also, if true, this is Texas's first moment of political change leading to a cultural shift in ways that fit general trends associated with demographic change. To this point in American history, Texas's independence has been observed because the state has confounded predictions of politics in urbanized and diverse states. The fact that the contraction of support for the Republican Party has also occurred during a period of economic prosperity calls for further explanation.

Our next chapter describes how Texas's two parties represent a new distribution of voters in each coalition. The electorate is sorting itself primarily based on ideology and race, suggesting an erosion of the effects that previously had Texas voters bucking prior assumptions. To investigate this further we look at the political preferences of voters by age, religion, and cultural identity.

In chapter 3 we discuss how political behavior and opinions in Texas vary based on the communities in which individuals live. Effectively, counties are the best level to understand why political change occurs faster in some communities of Texas than others. The rate of change is motivated by the economic realities, population change, and political traditions in each community. County election results reinforce that political change is being accelerated by the regions experiencing rapid population growth. One good example is Tarrant County, which voted for a Democratic candidate for the first time since 1964, supporting both Beto O'Rourke (2018) and Joe Biden (2020).

Chapters 4, 5, and 6 will address major moments that primed Texas voters to be enthusiastic about the 2020 election. Chapter 4 examines how Texas politicians have generated voter enthusiasm by promoting statism as they run for national office. The chapter also explains why Democratic candidates are more likely to expend effort in the future to seek support from Texas, as the largest delegate opportunity on Super Tuesday. Chapter 5 explains the limits progressive candidates like Bernie Sanders face in Texas based on below average turnout among some demographic groups and the excitement that can be generated for establishment Democrats from major events like the unique endorsement event with Senator Amy Klobuchar (D-MN) and Representative Beto O'Rourke on March 2, 2020. We then go on to discuss the double-edged benefit of stoking new voter enthusiasm to make a state a battleground in chapter 6. Record voter registration and turnout in Texas helped Democrats close the gap, but their advantages did not lead to a victory. We use our surveys and election results to track where voter turnout exceeded expectations and still fell below expectations in certain areas.

The shifting tides in electoral competition are reflective of the tensions that have emerged within the mass public in how residents evaluate the representation they are receiving from elected officials. The summer of 2020 contrasted the Lone Star state's deep tradition of prioritizing law and order with a reckoning about the importance of equality and opportunity. Chapter 7 expresses how the public's views on race and politics in Texas became malleable after the protests in cities across the state following the death of George Floyd, a man born in Houston, during an arrest in Minneapolis. Demands to end systemic racism from protestors and objections to any attempt to defund the police by candidates elevated the salience of race in Texas in tones that matched how immigration framed the 2018 elections, and the rhetoric by elites framed the debate of both as safety versus morality to split the electorate.

Another fascinating point about Texas politics during this time of change is the fragmentation of information sources. In the past decade, Texas has been home to the rise and end of Glenn Beck's cable TV channel the Blaze and other media companies have gained greater viewership. Chapter 8 reflects on our discussions about candidate choice and policy preference by asking, how do public perceptions vary in these different pockets that frame information differently? Are voters fragmented by their media consumption? This question is relevant to how media exposure and ideological diversity in the Republican Party frames how incumbents are viewed. State leaders such as Lieutenant Governor Dan Patrick choose to do media interviews only with Fox News, while Governor Abbott regularly conducts interviews with local television news stations. Moreover, a candidate like Beto O'Rourke made multiple media appearances across different outlets and mediums. In one of the most expensive media markets and second largest geographic state in the United States, how candidates reach voters is a significant barrier.

Our last chapter concludes the book with our understanding of how candidates are likely to influence how competitive the political parties in Texas will be moving forward. If parts of the public remain polarized, a candidate must attract support from Texas voters who do not strongly identify with a party to win. We see clear trends that suggest the personal characteristics of the candidate matter when attracting support from a diverse coalition of ethnicities and regions of the state.

CHAPTER 2

New Party Coalitions in Texas

We are at risk of turning purple. And if we don't do our job, then we could turn blue in the coming years.
—Senator John Cornyn in 2019

FOR MORE THAN TWO decades voters in Texas have supported the same party for president, governor, and the state legislature. This has allowed party identification in the state to be recognized as supporting the current leadership or not. Also, like much of the nation, partisanship often correlates with who someone will vote for. But for Texas, this assumption is more difficult to identify without a process of party registration and almost one in three voters refusing to identify with a party when asked.

The Republican advantage in Texas was built through pro-growth economic policies by Governors Bush, Perry, and Abbott. This success gave an edge to the faction of economic conservatives over members of the party who unabashedly prioritized socially conservative policies. The party had realized the advice from *Texas Monthly* columnist, Paul Burka: "[George W. Bush] is in a position to be a pivotal figure in Texas History, the person who leads the Republican party out of its brash Phil Gramm adolescence into maturity. But first he has to solve the same problem in Austin that Republicans now face in Washington: How to govern with a party whose elected officials hate government."[1] With President Trump in the White House, the brashness of national politics also changed Texas politics by emboldening a faction that was crucial to electing Senator Ted Cruz and Senator Phil Gramm before that.

In this chapter, we examine how diverse the party coalitions are for Texas Democrats and Texas Republicans in the contemporary period. Understanding the clear trends in the public's preference for a political party in Texas is valuable because it provides a point to compare what might happen if other states experience a population boom, especially among Latino and Asian voters. We discuss the nature of partisanship, but our intent is to also answer: Did party patterns change when Texas was reported to be a battleground state? The timeliness of our study coincided with Donald Trump's injection of a new populist movement to disrupt the Republican Party. We can look to whether the coalitions that have lasted for decades in Texas remained unchanged or identify the new balance of coalitions among Texas voters.

The shifts we see in the party identification of Texans mirror John R. Petrocik's description of the subsequent fracturing of the dominant Democratic Party coalition from the 1950s to the 1970s after the New Deal realignment in 1932. They also confirm the growing popularity of the minority party, which Wayne Thorburn, former executive director of the Republican Party of Texas observed in *Red State*.[2] In a new context, we can ask: What blocs of voters are important—and perhaps critical—to the Texas Democratic and Republican parties today? We also discuss ways the two major parties might go about broadening their respective voter bases going forward.[3]

What Is Partisanship and Why Is It Important?

The concept of partisanship is not difficult to understand at a surface level. Most people who decide to cast a vote on election day have a good idea of which candidates they are going to support, and typically those candidates bear the label of the Democratic Party or the Republican Party. Most voters will also, over time, develop a pattern of voting for the same party's candidates, particularly in highly visible, national elections like the presidential election. For these reasons, party identification is one of the more stable political variables; only shaken by dramatic political events or major changes in the life of the voter.[4] For most people ideology and partisan identification go hand in hand, because a voter either develops attitudes and opinions first (am I a liberal or a conservative?) or party identification first (am I a Democrat or am I a Republican?).[5] If these views are set as teams, we tend to see "our" party's candidates through rose-colored glasses and candidates from "that other party" as dastardly villains who could not possibly take reasonable positions on key issues.[6]

Republicans, Democrats, and Independents in Texas

We look at two of our preelection polls that took place immediately before the general elections of 2018 and 2020 to find that with respect to partisanship, Texas is politically divided like other states but with an advantage to Republicans. The timing of these snapshots is valuable because voters are most attentive to where they fall in the electorate just before an election, particularly those that are politically competitive. As can be seen in table 2.1, more than half the respondents in our preelection October polls in 2018 and 2020 identify as strong partisans in both years.[7] The largest group identify as strong Republicans (roughly 30%) in both years. Any suggestion that either party is likely to govern through compromise is challenged by the realization that there are so few moderates in the middle of the distribution. Parties are left to the strategy of trying to first break the association a voter has with the political party they currently prefer. Republican identifiers—lean, not strong, and strong—make up 47.8 percent of respondents in 2018 and 48.5 percent of respondents in 2020, while Democratic identifiers—lean, not strong, and strong—increased to 42.7 percent (in 2020) from 38.6 percent (in 2018). This gives Republican candidates an advantage of 6 to 10 percent in statewide elections, and that matches recent election results. The surprise of the 2020 election was how Republicans continued to hold the loyalty of its voters even as Texas Democrats made inroads with Independent voters. The increase in identification of both parties is evidence that voters are beginning to use more discernment when evaluating the political parties now that there is a viable alternative.

We also see great similarities in the public's party identification between 2018 and 2020, including the percentages of respondents who considered themselves to be strong or weak partisans—whether Democratic or Republican. Moreover, the increase in voters who admitted to leaning toward either the Democratic Party or the Republican Party, but still think of themselves as independent in 2020, is not surprising in the bright lights of the 2020 election. Viewed through the lens of the presidential election cycle, 2018 was a midterm election. The 2020 election was more visible, with President Trump facing off against former Vice President Biden, and it was held after Democratic primaries that included two Texas candidates. It is not surprising to see more Independents identify as independent "leaners" in 2020. Independents tend to have lower commitments to a political party, tend to be less engaged,

Table 2.1. Party Identification in Texas, Seven-Point Scale

	2018	2020
Party Identification	Percent	Percent
Strong Democrats	22.5%	22.1%
Weak Democrats	10.9	11.0
Democratic Leaners	5.2	9.6
Pure Independents	13.6	8.9
Republican Leaners	4.1	8.5
Weak Republicans	12.8	10.6
Strong Republicans	30.9	29.4
Total	100.0	100.0
	(n = 1031)	(n = 963)

tend to be less informed, tend to feel there is less at stake, and tend to turn out to vote at lower rates than partisans; but when pressed, many Independents will admit to leaning toward one party or the other, particularly near a national election.

In addition to the two surveys we conducted weeks before each election to capture the electorate in an easily comparable context, we conducted several other polls throughout the years of 2019, 2020, and 2021. These surveys are important to understand how perceptions of party identification change between elections. One point these studies bear out is that voters who at least leaned to the Democratic Party after Beto O'Rourke articulated a different path forward remained politically engaged in 2019 as he ran for president. During that time, the effort expended in the 2018 election left some Republicans in a malaise with their own party before events of 2020 and the contrast between National Democrats and Republicans brought them back to roost.

On the night of the election the chairman of the House Democratic Caucus Representative Chris Turner said, "Clearly we did not make the inroads we thought we would make."[8] To illustrate the Texas Democrats' "lost opportunity," the relative party identification advantage of Republicans over Democrats in Texas was 9.0 percent in 2018, but only 2.0 percent in the aggregate of our extensive polling in 2019. The Republicans' relative party identification advantage increased back to 8.3 percent in 2020 and remained at that level in 2021. Campaign consultants from both parties commented on the importance of building relationships with voters in Texas's new political climate. Democratic strategist Jeff Dalton gave another important perspective, "low-propensity voters sometimes need that personal touch. . . . We just didn't do canvassing like we would normally do. We simply did not." David Carney, chief consultant for Governor Greg Abbott, reinforced the advantage this gave Republicans by saying "people were dying to talk to people . . . they wanted to engage in our conversations" in short conversations at their front door.[9]

The excitement surrounding O'Rourke's presidential candidacy showed that Democrats could potentially compete in Texas if the Democratic base were excited and could rally around a popular Democratic candidate. After O'Rourke dropped out of the presidential race, even after he endorsed Joe Biden, the eventual Democratic nominee, it was business as usual in Texas. Cornyn won his race over MJ Hegar with a split in the two-party vote of 54.9 percent to 45.1 percent in the 2020 Senate race and Trump edged Biden by 52.8 percent to 47.2 percent of the two-party vote in in the presidential race in Texas. Both Republicans benefitted from a context where the thin Republican advantage in party identification in 2019 expanded back to the "normal" 9 percent advantage by October 2020, according to our polling. In retrospect, any acceleration of Texans identifying with the Democratic Party appears to be connected to whether Texas Democrats are visible on the national scene.

In Texas, the registered voters who are Independent and lean to one party are virtually indistinguishable from weak partisans in terms of supporting the party's candidates in elections.[10] This fact reinforces the notion that while a sizable number of respondents to any survey of Texas voters will claim to be Independent—and thus repelled from either political party —they really are a diverse group who are often more supportive of a party than they would like to admit. Pure Independents, who do not lean toward a party, exist but often participate in voting and other political behaviors at much lower rates than the leaners and partisans.[11]

Partisanship across Class, Identity, and Religion

The choice to be Democrat or a Republican is rooted in the experiences that frame a person's perspective about government. Children often adopt the partisanship of their parents. Socioeconomic characteristics, racial or ethnic identity, and religious identity frequently intersect how voters think about their representation and the ways parties express concern for challenges the public faces. Texas contradicts the national trend from the 1950s that people with higher levels of education tend to identify as Republicans and vice versa.[12] Registered voters who have a high school diploma or less only choose to identify as a Democrat (41%), 2 percent more often than they choose to at least lean toward the Republican Party. Texas Republicans maintain close to a 6 percent advantage in the party identification of those who attended some college or more. Texas Republicans also maintain stronger affinity with voters across all income brackets except for households making less than $50,000 per year. In the context of wealth in Texas, this is powerful because the median household income in the state was $64,304 in 2019. With Texas bucking the trend,[13] we infer class has been a stronger identifying feature of the party system in the United States than within individual states.[14] An explanation of why there is not more correlation between party identification and one's socioeconomic status as in the past is that Texans are making this decision based on culture and generational experiences.[15]

Race, ethnicity, and religious identification are other traditional features that have shaped the American party system since the New Deal realignment. African Americans tended to identify as Democrats during and after the New Deal, and they became even more strongly Democratic after passage of the 1964 Civil Rights Act and the 1965 Voting Rights Act.[16] This relationship holds in Texas, with the continued legacy of elected leaders like Representative Barbara Jordan, Representatives Al Green and Eddie Bernice Johnson who chaired committees in the U.S. House, and nationally recognized Mayors Ron Kirk and Sylvester Turner. The role of religion and partisanship is slightly more complicated in differences in how Catholics and Protestants behave as groups.

The two major parties in Texas are also noticeably divided by race. Figure 2.1 clearly reveals how party identification in Texas varies by each ideology within a race and ethnic category. Whites tend to identify as strong Republicans while African Americans identify as strong Democrats. More than half of the Latino respondents identified as Democrats, with 39.6 percent claiming to be strong Democrats in 2020. While Latinos are not as strongly tied to either of the two parties as are Blacks and Whites, it is not the case that Latinos all fall into the moderate or Independent category when it comes to party identification. In fact, only roughly 8 to 10 percent of Latinos identify as pure Independents. It is also significant that roughly 44 percent of Latinos express a preference for one party or the other, but are less likely to be strong

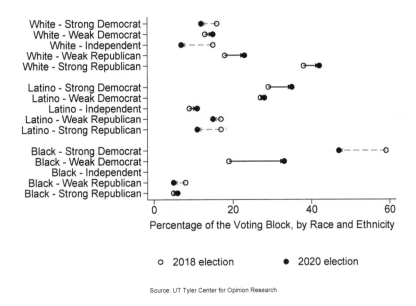

Figure 2.1. Change in Party Identification, by Race and Ethnicity, 2018 to 2020

partisans than Blacks or Whites in 2018 or 2020. The moderating effect is also emblematic of the expectation that Latino voters are more likely to identify as liberal than Anglo-Whites but are also more likely to hold policy views that are traditionally deemed conservative.[17]

The pattern from 2018 to 2020 is relatively stable, but there are intriguing shifts within each group. Fewer Whites identified as pure independents in 2020. As political tensions became more toxic, 7 percent fewer Blacks identify as strong partisans in 2020, but a whopping 13 percent more Blacks identify as weak Democrats or Democratic leaners in 2020. The overwhelming Democratic advantage among Black voters has not declined, but the ties to the Democratic Party do appear to be weaker. More Latinos began identifying as strong Democrats, and an only slightly smaller decrease in strong Republican identifiers. The relative Democratic advantage with Latino voters grew from 22.5 percent in 2018 to 37.3 percent after Trump's aggressive tone regarding the border wall and for increased hurdles to immigration from Latin America continued.

Religion is another cultural factor that influences political socialization.

Roman Catholics who immigrated to the United States during the nineteenth and early twentieth centuries tended to identify more with the Democrats than Protestants from the same social class. In Texas, this is also the case as 48 percent of Roman Catholics support the Democratic Party (6 percent more often than the Republican Party) during the time of our surveys. The overall trend is no different in Texas Protestants who have tended to support Republicans since the birth of the party in the 1850s, with the notable exception of White Southern Protestants who blamed the Republicans for their loss in the Civil War and did not forgive the Republicans for several decades for their role in Reconstruction.[18] In Texas, Protestants heavily favor the Republican Party and the advantage still exists if you consider the preferences of evangelicals (47% more Republican than Democratic) and mainline Protestants (26% more Republican than Democratic). The emphasis on protecting religion in Texas by Republicans has influenced the one in four Texans who have no religious affiliation at all to be more likely to support the Democratic Party.

The gradual realignment of White Southerners from the Democratic Party to the Republican Party through (political) "conversion," the movement of Rust Belt Republicans to the South, the generational replacement of old conservative Democrats by their grandchildren who were more likely to live in suburbs and be economically more comfortable, the growing tendency of Democrats to support civil rights (and social programs) for Black Americans, and the growth of a more prosperous White Southern middle-class, is well documented.[19] The massive movement of White evangelicals from the Democratic Party to the Republican Party from the 1980s to today, with the result that evangelicals are now more loyal Republicans than mainline Protestants, is also well documented.[20] We know also that in recent decades, there has been a gender gap, with women more likely to identify as Democrats when compared to men.[21]

Major Party Coalitions, 2018–2020

In his study of the New Deal coalition (that is, the Democratic Party, circa 1935–1975) John R. Petrocik illustrated how groups of voters (by characteristic) became more (or less) important to the Democratic Party as that voting group grew or decreased in size and support of the party during elections.[22] Petrocik's methodology offers a frame to analyze how ideology, as well as racial and ethnic identities affect the two major party coalitions in Texas today.

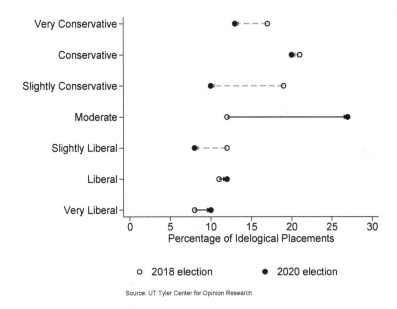

Figure 2.2. Ideological Self-Placement

Republicans have embraced the brand of conservatism to balance factions and Texas Democrats have sought to provide an alternative to those positions and give a voice to the most populous communities.[23] In figure 2.2 we can see how groups of registered voters are shifting in how they match different labels of ideology from 2018 to 2020.

Figure 2.2 confirms that Texas remains a conservative state, despite a two-fold increase in the percentage of moderates. In 2018, the gap between conservatives and liberal was 24.9 percent; in 2020, the gap in favor of conservatives was 13.5 percent. Part of the Republicans' advantage over Democrats in partisan identifiers is the advantage any conservative party would have in Texas.

In retrospect, the increase in moderates across the state is likely related to more registered voters who felt compelled to respond to a public opinion survey during a red-hot election season. The finding does not fundamentally mean that voters in the state all shifted to the left because there was not a substantial increase in the percentage of liberals. In 2020, the advantage was still to conservatives, but less so than in 2018. Not surprisingly, Whites tended to describe themselves as conservative, Blacks thought of themselves

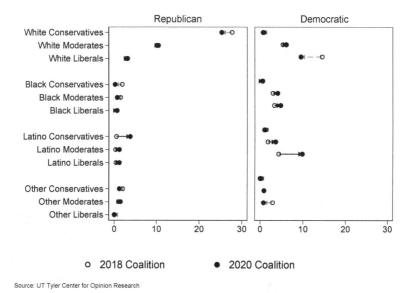

Figure 2.3. Party Coalitions, by Ideology and Race/Ethnicity

as liberal, and Latinos placed themselves mostly somewhere in the middle, but tending toward liberalism. The diversity of Texas's electorate allows us to compare how groups of voters are fit within the partisan coalitions based on race and ideology. The predominance of conservatism in Texas creates a skewed perspective about how a person might see themselves within a traditional ideological spectrum. We define these Texas liberals as anyone claiming to be "slightly" liberal or more as a liberal (a 1, 2, or 3 in our coding scheme); moderates as "moderate" or "slightly conservative;" and self-identified "conservative" or "very conservative" voters as a conservative. We report the party coalition results in figure 2.3.

The Republican Party coalition is largely made of up White respondents. Amazingly, 80.8 percent of respondents identifying as Republicans were either White conservatives or White moderates in 2018 and 2020. The percentage of Republicans who were conservative Latinos in the electorate did rise from 0.5 percent in 2018 to 3.8 percent in 2020. It is also notable that 28 White liberals identified as Republicans in 2018, which is 2.8 percent of all respondents of all voters; in 2020 the White liberals identifying as Republicans looked about the same. Figure 2.3 reveals that the Republican Party, for the most part, is not a multiethnic coalition of voters; instead, the Republican Party counts on overwhelming support from White Texans, both in terms of loyalty to the Republican Party and as a bloc of voters who is more likely than other groups to turn out to vote. The success of Republicans in state-wide elections cannot be denied, but it is evident that the Republican Party in Texas does have difficulty appealing to non-White voters.

The Democratic Party can better be described as a multiethnic coalition. Not just a party that appeals to racial and ethnic minorities, the Democratic Party also can count on White voters, to a degree. Whereas nearly 80 per-cent of Republicans come from only two voter coalition groups identified here, the Democrats rely on five different groups of voters. Democrats count White liberals, White moderates, Black liberals, Latino liberals, and Latino moderates as critical coalition groups within the party. This means Texas's Democratic Party has been trying to attract a wider base from 56 percent of registered voters we surveyed in the midterm election or 62 percent of 2020 voters. What one can see here is a true triethnic coalition, where White lib-erals and moderates make up 50.7 percent of Democratic Party identifiers in 2018 and 37.4 percent in 2020. It is also important to note that Latinos in our sample identified as Democrats over Republicans in 2018 and even more overwhelmingly in 2020.

Both parties have some challenges. Democrats rely on groups that turn out to vote at relatively low rates. Increasing the turnout of Blacks, Latinos, and moderate White voters who identify as Democrats is essential for the Demo-crats. Given the size of the moderate White voting bloc, Democrats need to do better than attracting only roughly 40 percent of members of that bloc who identify as partisans as well as the substantial numbers of White moder-ates who identify as independents.

The challenge for Republicans is to win the allegiance of as many non-White voters as possible, particularly those who identify as conservatives. Our survey results, and recent history in Texas, including bitter debates in the legislature about what to do about Confederate monuments and voting in the state, sug-gest that it will be difficult for Republicans to garner substantial percentages of African American voters in the near future.[24] Given the demographic realities of the future, both parties will need to court Latino voters. One observer of the U.S. Census Bureau numbers released in late August 2020 stated: "Since 2010, the state has gained eleven new Latino residents and three new Black res-idents for every non-Hispanic White."[25] Republicans must appeal to more than

40 percent of the Latino voting bloc, or it will be difficult for Republicans to consistently win statewide races. The mirror of that story is true for Democrats; if Republicans can improve their standing with moderate Latinos and continue to win the support of most White moderates, the Democratic Party in Texas will be isolated as a metropolitan-based party.

A Republican agenda that emphasizes ideology over race is not without its own controversy. Opponents have increasingly brought forth allegations that actions by the Texas Republicans in the government disadvantage the representation of people of color in the state from redistricting to judicial elections. The frequency of this claim makes it more difficult for Republicans to court Latino voters. Following this logic, several Latino voters and a community group initiated a legal challenge in 2016 on the use of partisan elections to select appellate judges in the state of Texas. The legal challenge claimed that partisan elections reduced minority voting rights in violation of the 1965 Civil Rights Act, similar to past legal challenges brought by African Americans. The final ruling was that partisan elections were not disadvantageous to the representation of Latino voters in elections for the state appellate court, but the deliberation highlighted the fact that Republicans are sometimes seen as being blind to the needs of minority populations in the state.[26]

The well of unaffiliated voters in Texas is small and their views are unpredictable. It is important to remember "pure" Independents in Texas are the least likely to turn out to vote. The incentive for parties to put in the hard work to increase engagement with true Independents is the chance that they may become "leaners" or weak partisans and create momentum for the future. The process of realizing these changes is underway. Our surveys of the 2020 electorate found a precipitous increase in White moderates leaning to one of the two parties, when compared to 2018, and a decrease in the percentage of Latino moderates and Asians willing to identify with a party. Seeing swing voters and an emerging Asian electorate shift in different directions captures the trade-offs and consequences of efforts to bind together a coalition to support the party in power.

A Final Note: Partisanship Revisited

Ideology and race often influence whether a voter has a sense of belonging with a political party, but associations can differ by gender, income, marital status, and income. Using those characteristics just listed, we want to explain why voters choose their partisanship across the range from strong Democrats to strong Republicans. Our descriptions reflect the findings from a multinomial logistic regression model of a voter's choice to identify as a strong Democrat, weak or leaning to the Democratic Party, pure Independents, weak or leaning Republicans, and strong Republicans.[27] The model selection is important because voters do not necessarily weaken in their party affiliation before they move. They could just as easily move from a strong partisan to a pure Independent and become a partisan through a strong connection to a candidate.

The results of the model reveal ideology, income, race, and religion are significantly shaping partisanship within the Texas electorate. The influence of ideology is straightforward and consistent. Conservative voters often identify as strong Republicans more than any other category during the entire time period. Income has marginally affected individual's choice to identify with a party in 2018 and again after the Trump presidency. Regarding race, Latinos are identifying with the Democratic Party more often, but all races are becoming less attached to whichever party they chose than in 2018. Another recognizable shift is that mainline Protestant Christians are no longer significantly more likely to identify as strong Republicans than weak Republicans or Democrats. We will describe how likely voters are to select their identification across the party scale by comparing choices made in 2018, 2019, 2020, and 2021.

The intentional outreach of Texas Democrats to create an ethnically diverse coalition has grown the party without driving Whites and Latinos from the party. Blacks remain less likely than "other races" to identify as Republicans (or more likely to identify as Democrats). The tensions between Black voters and the Texas Republican Party have calcified from public statements by elected leaders like Lieutenant Governor Dan Patrick who deflected blame from a wave of coronavirus hospitalizations by saying: "The biggest group in most states are African Americans who have not been vaccinated. The last time I checked over 90 percent of them [Blacks] vote for Democrats."[28] The survey respondents we have spoken to from 2018 to 2021 were significantly more likely to identify as either a strong or weak Democrat more than a strong Republican. There was no statistical difference among Black voters in their choice to be Independent, weak Republican or strong Republican when you control for other characteristics. The bar chart in figure 2.4 shows how party identification choices have been distributed by race across this time period.

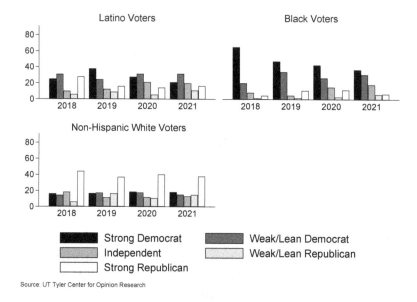

Figure 2.4. Strength of Partisanship, by Race and Ethnicity

Latino voters have awakened within the Texas electorate as they receive more attention from candidates. Latino voters have always turned out at the same rate as other races, but the ethnic group did have lower levels of voter registration prior to the 2018 and 2020 elections. This period was pivotal for Texas politics because of the meteoric 9 percent rise of Latinos in the electorate from 2016 to 2020 (16 to 25 percent of all registered voters). The change was twofold, more individuals entering the voting age population were Latino and activity related to both elections introduced 1.8 million more registered voters in Texas. Our surveys found that the newly expanded Latino electorate did not have a decided partisan tilt in 2018, but Latinos were significantly more likely to identify as Democrats by 2020. This reflects a reduction in the percentage of Latino voters who identified as Republicans as President Trump sought reelection and a slow increase in Latino voters willing to identify as weak Republicans in 2021.

After controlling for ideology, income, age, and religion, the affinity of White voters for the two parties is an interesting relationship. White voters are neither significantly more likely nor less likely to identify as strong Democrats than strong Republicans, all else equal. White voters are still more likely to indicate they are strong Republicans than say they are pure Independents or Independents who lean to the Democratic Party, which appropriately reflects how many White voters indicated they were conservative. The modest erosion of White strong Republicans has the potential to have major implications for how we think about Texas politics going forward, unless the intense support for the Republican Party exceeds levels from 2018.

Race and ethnicity certainly play a role in how partisanship is framed and viewed in the state. What might surprise many is the new trend where White voters now make up less of the electorate and affiliate with the Republican Party slightly less. The trends also clarify an important point about how Texas has become a state where slightly less than 60 percent of White voters identify with or lean toward the Republican Party, an opposite circumstance than the partisan divide within the White population in the 1940s that favored the Democrats. The key to how race matters in Texas may be better understood as the interaction between policies, actions, and ideology that we describe in a later chapter.

Texas has been isolated from political changes as a result of generational shifts for a long time, but the emerging bloc of voters ages eighteen to twenty-four appear to be at odds with the larger voting bloc of voters ages sixty-five years and older. Beneath the contrast of extremes, a consequential shift has also been the decreasing intensity of identification with the Republican Party among voters ages twenty-five to forty-five since 2018. In 2019, among voters ages twenty-five to thirty-four strong Republican was no longer the most common affiliation and voters were just as likely to identify as weak Democrats and Independents as they were to identify as strong Republicans. This shift for voters between the ages of thirty-five and forty-four occurred a year later when the youngest of Gen X and oldest millennials were more likely to identify as strong Democrats than strong Republicans. This distinction largely came from a drop in how frequently these voters identified as strong Republicans, making the selection more in line with all other levels of partisanship. By 2021, the scale of partisanship began to tilt left with voters of every age group more likely to identify as a strong Democrat than a strong Republican after controlling for factors such as ideology, demography, and socioeconomic indicators.

Socioeconomic effects on partisanship in Texas have been volatile in the 2020s. The expectation that voters with higher education are more likely to

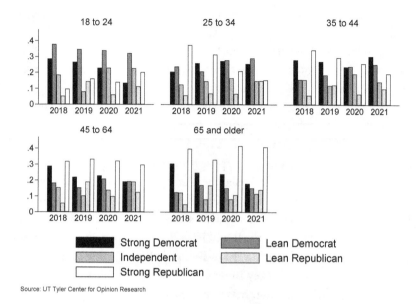

Figure 2.5. Strength of Partisan Identification in Texas, by Age

identify with the Democratic Party did not fit Texas well, until 2021. One of the reasons is Texas has a robust junior college system, and in many cases the boom-and-bust industries in the state offer high wages without requiring a college degree. In good times, one will rarely find significant variation in partisanship based on level of education as we saw in 2018. In 2019, voters with a college degree became more likely to identify as weak Democrats than strong Republicans. That relationship did not exist in 2020, but voters with a college degree were more likely to identify as weak Republicans than strong Republicans. The shift in partisanship among voters with a college degree in 2021, when degree holders were more likely to identify as any Democrat more than a strong Republican, gives us a new starting point to think about the impact of education in Texas. The effect of education began to challenge ideology to diminish the intensity of support college educated voters had given to the Republican Party. The shift happened after Texas Democrats achieved the goal of winning Texas's six most populous counties and the Texas government began defying the federal government during the start of the Biden administration.

Year to year, household income is strongly correlated with partisanship, with wealthier respondents identifying as Republicans and lower-income respondents identifying as Democrats. The period between 2018 and 2021 offers a fascinating context to think about this relationship because Texas experienced record low unemployment in 2019 and record high unemployment in 2020. In 2019, voters with higher levels of wealth were just as likely to identify as Independent or Republican and less likely to identify as Democratic. In 2020, the relationship between wealth and partisanship only predicted that voters with more wealth would identify as strong Republicans more often than strong Democrats, all other choices were not statistically different. In 2021, the difference in voters identifying as a strong Republican more than a strong Democrat based on wealth was no longer apparent. Voters with less income and more income were just as likely to associate with either party, but the interesting trend is that voters were more committed in that choice. Fewer voters identified themselves as weak Democrats or Independents at higher levels of income. Income is a variable that often affects politics in the short term, because it is how voters are able to easily evaluate in retrospect for how well the voter is doing now.[29] These were factors that helped explain partisan identification before 2000 but are much weaker associations in the complexity of today's politics in Texas.

Religion has been a powerful cultural divide in how voters in Texas think of themselves as partisans. The prioritization of Christian values by Texas Republicans has set clear paths within religious denominations for voters to follow toward the party. Evangelical voters are more likely to be strong Republicans than weak Democrats or Independents. The connection grows more strongly in election years when evangelicals in Texas identify as strong Republicans more often than strong Democrats. Roman Catholics in the state were no more likely to be a strong Republicans more than any other level of partisanship in 2018 or 2019. The 2020 election set an edge where Catholic voters were significantly more likely to identify as strong Republicans more than all other classifications of partisanship. The slight advantage for Republicans with voters of the Catholic faith was no longer evident in 2021, but Catholics were more likely to identify as strong Republicans than Independents reflecting the separation we expect from close party competition. The relationship between mainline Protestant Christians and the Republican Party in Texas appears to be strained. Mainline Protestants have not more likely identified as Republicans than Democrats since 2018, and voters of these faiths were even more likely to identify as Democratic supporters than strong Republicans in 2019 during the crowded Democratic presidential primaries. In summary, what our analysis in this chapter shows is that Republicans are the dominant party, but some core constituencies of the Bush-led coalition that won the state are reevaluating their place in this coalition. The Republicans clear benefit is the fact that more citizens in the state think of themselves as conservatives than as liberals, which is engrained in the state's historical political culture. Changing demographics will force Republicans to find ways to heal the strained sense of belonging that Latino voters and White moderates have with political parties in Texas; whichever party can do this will continue to win elections in the future.[30]

CHAPTER 3

Lone Star Split

Regional Political Identities

If you've ever driven across Texas, you know how different one area of the state can be from another. Take El Paso. It looks as much like Dallas as I look like Jack Nicklaus.
—Lee Trevino[1]

I N FRONT OF THE Smith County Courthouse on the top of a double decker bus, Senator John Cornyn stoked a crowd of supporters before the 2020 election saying, "We are depending on Tyler, Smith County and East Texas to win this, . . . if it hadn't been for places like East Texas coming in 2 to 1, [Senator Cruz] might not have won that race [in 2018], it was less than 3 points. We need everyone to get out and vote and take all your friends and family with you." During this campaign stop in Tyler on October 29, 2020, the senior senator, who was seeking his own reelection, was urgently trying to get out the vote in areas of the state where Republicans traditionally won by larger margins.[2]

The election would later prove Cornyn's statement was prophetic for the outcome of the election. Voter turnout in East and West Texas was large enough to cover the Democratic advantage in the largest metropolitan areas. President Trump's strongest support came from counties in metropolitan areas with fewer than 250,000 people. Those counties are largely located in East Texas where communities are smaller and more spread out. As for counties in areas with more than 250,000 residents, President Trump received strong support in Lubbock but weak support in El Paso. Another worthy comparison is that seven communities with this population density had turnout over the state average and eighteen did not. Communities around Amarillo in the panhandle had the highest voter turnout in 2020 and Laredo (Webb County) had the lowest turnout of 50 percent in the 2020 election.

Joe Biden's narrow advantage in Tarrant County, where Fort Worth is the county seat, showed that meaningful political changes had occurred in Texas. A Democratic nominee for president had not received the most votes in Tarrant County since native son Lyndon Johnson did so against Republican Barry Goldwater. Biden's success also showed that a Democratic candidate could repeat the success of Beto O'Rourke's candidacy by attracting new support in this growing and populated county.

The partisan balance of voters in each of these counties is unique and add layers of complexity to a candidate's strategy of how to win Texas. Distinguishing between major metropolitan areas, large cities, midsize cities, and small town or rural areas offers four levels of urbanization to understand how Texas reflects America. These distinct communities have been pivotal to elections in Texas at different times. Observing political change at the county level uncovers the nuances in how Texas is always changing. The changes are not always in the same direction, which masks the expedience of a politically responsive state.

A Political Gap between Urban and Rural Texas

In the past twenty-eight years of Texas's political history more and more votes have been coming from the largest population centers. Such a trend of urbanization is often identified as a primary mechanism for political change, particularly with respect to partisan competition.[3] As more of a state's voters live in select metropolitan areas political parties adapt to be the voice of the majority or of the state's tradition. These effects are most commonly seen when a state's politics are described as dots of blue in a sea of red. Texas has numerous distinct dots, but much of the attention is placed on Austin, Dallas, Fort Worth, Houston, and San Antonio. The thirty-five counties in those five distinct metropolitan areas account for 67 percent of Texas's registered voters and in the 2020 election made up 70 percent of all ballots cast. The 172 counties that the census defines as not-metropolitan areas account for about 11 percent of all registered voters and ballots cast in the election.

The votes cast in the 2020 presidential election show that a Democratic candidate held a 5 percent advantage over the Republican incumbent for all

Table 3.1. Distribution of Counties by Level of Urbanization in 2020

Level	Number of Counties	Pct. of Reg. Voters	Pct. Early Votes	Pct. Election Day Votes	Trump Adv. In 2020
Metro: 1 million or more	35	67%	71%	70%	D +5%
Metro: 250,000 to 1 million	25	15	13	13	R +3
Metro: 250,000 or less	22	8	6	6	R +43
Small Town - Rural	172	10	10	11	R +52

votes cast in the thirty-five major urban counties (table 3.1). Among voters in the small towns and rural areas of Texas, noted as the 172 counties we just mentioned, the party split greatly favored Republicans, 52 percent (23% D; 75% R). The party division between the most urban and least urban communities is notable, because the votes that Donald Trump received over Joe Biden in the small towns and rural areas of Texas was 5.7 percent of all votes cast in the state. The final difference in the election was that Donald Trump Received 5.6 percent more votes than Joe Biden.

The trend toward urbanization has been building in all areas of the state, but most notably in Dallas and Houston, Texas's two largest cities, have had the greatest impact. From the time that George H. W. Bush ran for reelection in 1992 to today, Dallas has continued to have higher voter turnout than the state and now makes up 2 percent more of the state's electorate. Turnout in Houston has fluctuated year to year on whether it keeps pace with the state average, but despite being responsible for 1 percent more of the state's electorate in 2020, it produced 3 percent more of the state's votes than 1992. Figure 3.1 points to the recent leverage that Austin achieved in the 2020 election after widespread voter registration drives following the 2018 election. The deep shades of the counties in the map reflects the extent those votes favored the Democrats. Conversely, the relative height of the county shape to those of Bexar (to the South), Dallas (to the North), and Harris (to the East) show that the pro-Democratic ballots only go so far given the partisan balance of other metropolitan areas.

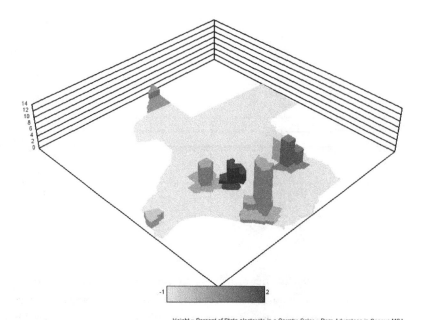

Height = Percent of State electorate in a County; Color = Dem Advantage in Census MSA

Fig 3.1. Distribution of Texas's Votes in Large Metropolitan Areas, 2020

The ebb and flow of where new residents of the state are moving to, voter turnout, and shifts in candidate preference have produced a different political geography when we compare 1992 to 2020. The three maps below show the story by visualizing all of Texas's 254 counties at different points in time: 1992, 2000, and 2020. The 1992 election is an important moment to begin our comparison because all statewide offices were held by Democrats and Republicans had a relative advantage over Democrats in the urban areas. The uniqueness of Ross Perot's popularity in Texas as a contrast to the Democratic Party and Republican establishment certainly adds a twist but gives a glimpse of where partisan defections were likely to occur. In the map (figure 3.2), counties are shaded darker when Democratic nominee Bill Clinton received a higher share of the vote, counties are lighter when Vice President George H. W. Bush received the most votes, and diagonal stripes represent the three counties that Ross Perot led the three-way split of the votes. The comparison reminds us that the North Texas counties surrounding Dallas all favored Republicans in the 1990s and the Democratic advantage was strongest

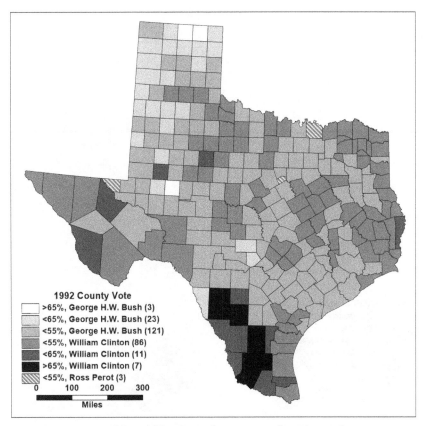

Figure 3.2. Candidate Preference in the 1992 Presidential Race, by County

in South Texas and El Paso. The remarkable difference between then and now is that Bush's relative advantage over Clinton in all counties was low (as seen by the numerous gray counties).

The candidacy of Texas Governor George W. Bush for president shows the clearest advantage for Republicans across Texas's counties. Another lesson is that the relative advantage for Republicans in the urban areas did not increase as it did elsewhere. The counties within the Dallas–Fort Worth metroplex favored the Republican, while the I-35 corridor (Bexar, Hays, and Travis) remained competitive as voters chose between Governor Bush and Vice President Al Gore. The map of the 2000 election (figure 3.3) also shows that the narrative of George W. Bush appealing to Latino voters may

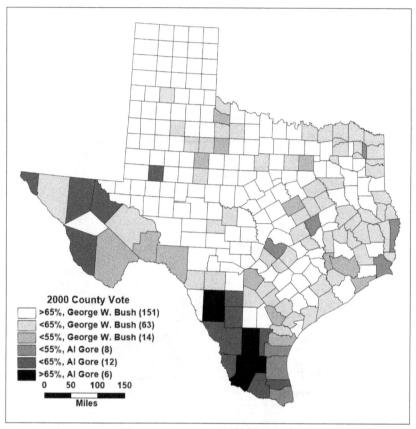

Figure 3.3. Candidate Preference in the 2000 Presidential Race, by County

not have extended to El Paso and the Rio Grande Valley. The preferences of those geographic areas remained strongly aligned with the Democratic candidate.

Geographically, the 2020 election shows that votes from the counties in Texas were quite different than the past (figure 3.4). The number of counties to support the Democratic nominee declined in the West, East, and South Texas except for counties with the largest population centers. We also see a stark contrast to the election from twenty years before, because with former Vice President Joe Biden the Democratic candidate held a much stronger advantage over the Republican incumbent in the urban centers and along the I-35 corridor. Our consistent surveys of Texas voters between 2018 and 2021

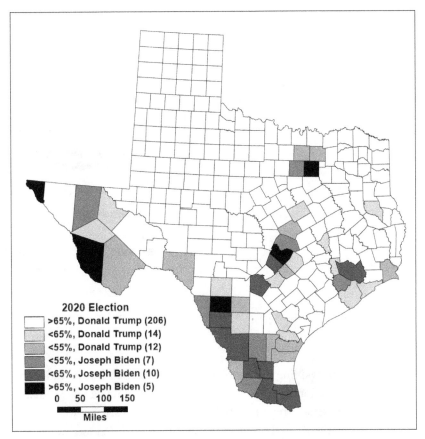

2020 Election
>65%, Donald Trump (206)
<65%, Donald Trump (14)
<55%, Donald Trump (12)
<55%, Joseph Biden (7)
<65%, Joseph Biden (10)
>65%, Joseph Biden (5)
0   50 100 150
Miles

Figure 3.4. Candidate Preference in the 2020 Presidential Race, by County

provide an opportunity to pool those studies together and get a more robust comparison of shifts in partisanship and policy views between the elections.

Figure 3.5 looks at voters who live in communities with similar population density to compare how these shifts in the partisan identification of voters varied each year. The largest cities and the counties that surround them have favored the Republican Party, yet during that same time registered voters from the areas of more than one million residents favored Joe Biden over Donald Trump by 6 percent in 2020. This break occurred in 2020, because urban voters were largely split between the two candidates in 2019.

As we look to smaller communities, it seems that voters in metro areas with 250,000 to one million residents—like El Paso and Waco—registered

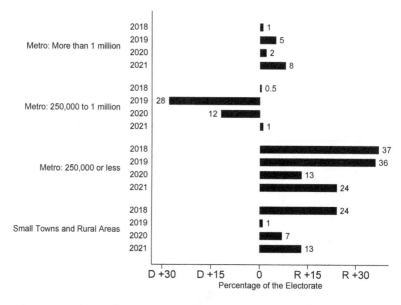

Figure 3.5: Party Advantage Among Registered Voters, by Urbanization

voters in Texas are waffling in the strength of their partisanship. Ahead of the 2018 midterm election, registered voters in these communities were equally divided in their partisanship (+ 0.5% R). In 2019 and 2020, fewer were willing to identify with the Republican Party and favored Joe Biden by 6 percent in during the months preceding the 2020 election. Despite the potential for political change, the ballots cast from these counties favored Donald Trump by 3 percent. But perhaps the most surprising point is to look back at the small town and rural communities that President Trump won with a 52 percent advantage. Registered voters in small towns across Texas are not nearly as Republican in their personal party identification as the election outcomes might imply. The dilemma is, to what extent are Democratic voters in the smaller metro areas and small towns disaffected by the political process?

The challenge for Democratic candidates to capitalize on the urban advantage reflects lower than average turnout of voters who would support a Democratic candidate in the rest of the state. Perhaps more important than recognizing the national attention to Loving County's 111 registered voters for supporting President Trump at a higher percentage than any other county in the nation, voter turnout in counties with populations smaller than one million and larger than 250,000 was 2 percent lower than the state average. These twenty-five counties are major economic hubs in different regions, like El Paso, Edinburgh/McAllen, Lubbock, Beaumont, and Waco. Votes in these counties favored incumbent President Donald Trump by 3 percent, even though surveys from the *Dallas Morning News* and University of Texas at Tyler estimate that Democrats have a 1 percent advantage in the partisan identification of registered voters. As the population size of communities gets smaller, the differential between actual vote share and the partisanship of survey respondents continues to grow.

In the smallest metropolitan areas like Tyler and Midland-Odessa, metropolitan areas have fewer than 250,000 residents. It is rare for Democratic candidates to invest time and resources in the communities, because 8 percent of the electorate lives in these communities and the Republican Party is better organized in the communities. What is striking is that the Republican advantage at the ballot box (R +43%) is almost two to one more than what we found by asking survey respondents in these counties what their partisanship was (R +16%). The severe lag in turnout for Democratic voters persists through the rest of the rural continuum for counties that are nonmetropolitan but adjacent to a metropolitan area, like Athens, Texas in Henderson County, or the previously mentioned Loving County that is completely rural.

This chapter will identify how urbanization and the political culture of regions in the state affect elections by using Texas's election returns from 1992 to 2020 and our comprehensive database of surveys conducted from 2018 to 2021. The longitudinal differences in election results and survey data show the rate of political change within the state has not been consistent for each region or level of urbanization when we aggregate information from counties to the region. This leads us to ask: How does political participation vary by region? What are the political consequences of Texas's distinct political regions?

How Do Regions in Texas Differ Politically?

The individualism of Texas politics is reinforced by the unique cultural identities of communities within the state. Ten distinct political regions (if one counts Dallas and Fort Worth in the same region) reflect the five major metropolitan areas and five additional regions with similar economic ties. Houston and Dallas are the two largest metropolitan areas and San Antonio, Fort Worth, and Austin are similar in their population sizes when you consider the neighboring counties. East Texas, El Paso, Hill Country, Southeast Texas, the Valley, and West Texas have their own political identities that are distinct from other regions and the major metro areas. The distinctions between these ten regions help us understand the variation that exists across the state's 254 counties.

An examination of Texas politics at the regional level tells the story that the speed of political change in Texas varies by county and region. The boundaries of the regions are set by the United States Office of Management and Budget and categorizes Texas's 254 counties into twenty-seven different metropolitan areas (or divisions) and forty-four micropolitan areas. The OMB also differentiates the metropolitan areas by the size of the population of the geographically proximate counties.[4] The urban-rural continuum sets a clear measure to compare geographic areas with those of similar population size. Metropolitan areas can also be differentiated as a population of more than one million, more than 250,000, and metropolitan areas more than twenty thousand. Other classifications are used to identify communities that are not metropolitan or rural.

Across the nation, and particularly in the South, urbanization has shaped the diversity of politics within a state. Texas is no different. Two-thirds of registered voters in Texas live within Houston, Dallas, Fort Worth, San Antonio, and Austin metropolitan areas. The multiple metropolises across the state make the state unique because communities are geographically distant from one another and urban sprawl makes each metropolis less centralized. Moreover, six of the fifteen fastest growing large cities in America between 2010 and 2019 were in Texas. The Texas cities exploding in population size were Frisco (71%), New Braunfels (56%), McKinney (52%), Cedar Park (44%), Conroe (39%), and Round Rock (33.3%). Interestingly, none of these cities are the center of their own metropolitan area. Frisco and McKinney are adjacent to Dallas. Austin is a prime attraction for growth in the adjacent cities of Cedar Park and Round Rock. New Braunfels is close in proximity to San Antonio and Conroe is to the north of Houston. This presents a clear dichotomy where Dallas, Houston, and Austin have moved faster to the Democratic Party and Texas's fastest growing areas like Frisco, Conroe, and Cedar Park have been reliably Republican. The partisan contrasts within the same local geographic area provide a regional example of Clayton Nall's observation that the development of the highway system contributed to political polarization by allowing residents to sort themselves into new communities.[5]

Geographic differences within each metropolitan area muted the dominance of Democratic candidates across Texas's largest urban areas in elections prior to 2018. The 10 percent advantage Democratic candidates receive from Harris County would have less leverage in a statewide election because Republican candidates also drew strong support from the Houston area in Montgomery County. For campaigns, appealing to urban centers becomes increasingly more expensive because each geographically dispersed metropolitan area has its own large media market and there are twenty different viewing markets in the state. The 2020 election marked a unique moment where the Democratic nominee for president won all five metropolitan areas for the first time since 1976. In fact, the election results showed how different these thirty-five counties are from the rest of the state as Joe Biden (D) received 5 percent more of the votes than Donald Trump (R). Our frequent surveys of the state estimate national Democratic candidates are still underperforming in Texas's urban areas with more than 7 percent of registered voters identifying or leaning more toward the Democratic Party than the Republican Party.

Are the Regions of Texas Politically Distinct?

Texas communities are at times described as metroplexes, borderplexes, cities, and towns in order to distinguish how one settlement of residents is different from others nearby or those in the state with similar population sizes. Nevertheless, 70 percent of all votes cast in the 2020 election came from Texas's five largest metropolitan areas. As some of these areas are growing faster than the rest of the country, the biggest question for the future of Texas's politics is how will elections change as other metropolitan areas become more urbanized?

The metroplex designation captures the broader identity of a population centered around a city that has sprawled beyond the municipal and county boundaries. The sprawl from the large metroplexes, especially after the mid-2000s, has blurred the demarcations that once clearly separated one seat of county government from another, like Austin and Round Rock, San Antonio, and New Braunfels, or most notably Dallas and Fort Worth. A deeper look at the metroplexes, especially those along I-35 and population centers along the U.S.-Mexico border, shows how these communities differ politically.

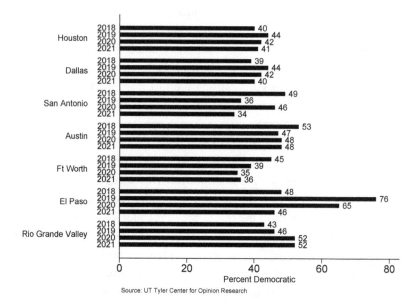

Figure 3.6: Annual Percentage of Voters Identifying With the Democratic Party, by Metropolitan Area

Houston

The Greater Houston metropolitan area is the fifth most populated community in the nation. The city, along the bayous and channel to the Gulf of Mexico, is economically prosperous as the home to many major energy companies and NASA's mission control. The sprawl of residents drawn to Houston spreads across nine counties that include Harris County as the primary population center, and the counties of Fort Bend, Montgomery, Brazoria, Galveston, Chambers, Liberty, Waller, and Austin. Within those counties, the Woodlands and Sugar Land continue to be among the fastest growing cities in America and also contrast with the more Democratic Harris County.

The partisan differences between Harris County and the rest of Greater Houston illustrate many traits associated with partisan sorting.[6] Democratic candidates have the strongest advantage with voters in Harris County, who identify with the Democratic Party most often (46% D; 41% R). A partisan advantage for Republicans in the surrounding counties persisted (36% D; 53% R). The population growth outside of Houston proper and the partisan differences of these communities gives the Republican Party a 4 percent advantage in the partisan identification of registered voters in the Greater Houston area. The competitiveness of both parties within the region stokes higher than usual voter turnout that soaked the Houston area with 24 percent of all ballots cast in Texas during the 2020 election despite the state having 23 percent of all registered voters.

The complexity of Houston's politics goes beyond partisan identification, because of the international influence in the city from those drawn from different parts of the United States, Central America, Asia, and elsewhere. In the Greater Houston area, a majority of Black (70% D; 16% R) and Latino (54% D; 29% R) voters identify or lean toward the Democratic Party. Conversely, most White voters identify with the Republican Party (30% D; 62% R). As the Asian population of Houston continues to grow, so does its ability to affect politics in the region. Asian voters in Houston, who are largely of Chinese and Vietnamese descent, are split in their partisan identification (35% D; 46% R).

Houston's 2.3 million households makes it the eighth largest media market in the nation. The battle for a political advantage in any election becomes a contest between candidates for a marginal share of the geographic and ethnic diversity of the region. Moreover, Joe Biden's ability to carry the Greater Houston area, despite the Republican advantage among registered voters, suggests that another important margin exists with the voters in the region who feel only a weak connection to the national leaders of the party. The careers of Houstonians like President George H. W. Bush and Senator Ted Cruz illustrate how unlocking the puzzle of Houston voters is vital to the political power of the state.

Dallas–Fort Worth: Two Divisions

The Dallas–Fort Worth metroplex is larger than Houston, representing 25 percent of the registered voters in the state of Texas. Both major cities share the same media market, meaning that voters who primarily get their information from a television are likely to receive the same options across the almost 2.6 million households in the fifth largest media market in the nation. Fort Worth is the thirteenth largest city in the United States as of 2021, and Dallas is the ninth largest city in the nation when the cities of the metroplex are considered separately.

The proximity of these cities often overshadows the distinct cultures between these areas. To say they are as far apart as Deep Ellum and the Stockyards might be an overstatement, but census data delineate the larger metroplex into two different metropolitan divisions that have had different economic histories and voting patterns. Most notably in 2016, Fort Worth was the largest metropolitan area to reliably support Republican candidates. Fort Worth's metro area was even more Republican as it includes counties on the west side of the metroplex (Johnson, Parker, and Wise) in addition to Tarrant County that includes Fort Worth and Arlington.

Politically, Tarrant County is now extremely competitive after it showed slight support for Beto O'Rourke (D) in 2018 and Joe Biden (D) in 2020. The recent retirement of Mayor Betsy Price (R), who won five consecutive elections, raised a new question: How strongly do voters still support Republicans in Fort Worth? Our tracking of the partisanship of voters by metro area (figure 3.5) shows that Republicans have a double-digit advantage in the party affiliation of registered voters in the Fort Worth metro area. If you compare the densely populated Tarrant County to the other three counties that define the Fort Worth metropolitan division, the Republican advantage holds across the region. We estimate 9 percent more of the registered voters in Tarrant County identify as Republicans as compared to Democrats (39% D; 48% R), and the advantage is even greater outside in the surrounding counties (29% D; 60% R).

The contrast of voters in Tarrant County to the surrounding areas also becomes clear when we consider how the voters approve of leaders. In Johnson, Parker, and Wise counties, voters consistently rewarded President Trump with job approval ratings of 69 percent in 2019 and 66 percent in 2020. If we contrast the approval rating of President Trump with Governor Greg Abbott, the governor received an additional 8 percent bump in this more conservative area and a 10 percent bump in Tarrant County (49% Trump; 59% Abbott). The elevated approval numbers for Governor Abbott across the region, compared to the president, largely show how Independent voters in this area respond to different leadership styles.

On the eastside of the metroplex, Dallas County is a Democratic anchor for a metro division that includes six other counties that balances the partisanship of the region. The partisan lean of surrounding counties is an almost exact counterweight to Dallas leaving the larger region with a 4 percent advantage for Republicans among all registered voters (42% D; 46% R). In

Dallas County, the voters we surveyed favored the Democratic Party by 18 percent (52% D; 34% R). The Republican advantage exists in the surrounding communities like Frisco, Plano, and McKinney and is 21 percent (33% D; 54% R). As the populations of those communities grow by attracting highly educated and high-income residents, Democratic candidates are attracting support where they had not been able to before.

Like the Fort Worth area, voters in the Dallas area approved of Governor Greg Abbott more than President Donald Trump by more than double digits. In 2020, Governor Abbott maintained an average job approval of 53 percent in the region; 48 percent in Dallas and 59 percent in the surrounding counties. In the same time frame, President Trump's approval in the Dallas area (41%) was lower than the state average and did not eclipse 50 percent in the surrounding counties. President Trump's declining popularity was lowered by the disapproval of Latino voters (75%), Black voters (64%), and Asian voters (63%) in Dallas County. President Trump's approval was primarily registered with White voters in Dallas (52%) and its surrounding counties (57%). The future of North Texas's influence on politics may be tied to how quickly political change in Fort Worth, Plano, or Dallas occurs. Across the board voters are less likely to turn away from supporting traditional Republicans, which reinforces the expectation that candidate characteristics are a strong predictor about the future more than partisanship.

I-35 Corridor

As I-35 runs north from Laredo, through Austin, up to Dallas, and continues into Oklahoma, the interstate is the vehicle by which communities in Texas are blending. There is not a rural portion of I-35, even if communities within ten miles of the interstate can be quite rural. Another important reason to think about I-35 as a major demarcation in Texas is that it serves as the point in which communities in Texas lose the influence of the traditional South. Traveling from east to west across the state one will notice that the towering pine trees become non-existent an hour before you reach I-35 in Dallas, and the landscape becomes a mix of brush and oak trees. An hour west of I-35, the elevation of Texas changes with valleys and plateaus that give the Texas Hill Country its name and beauty. Yet it is between those pine forests and hill country that most of Texas's population growth and political change is occurring.

Austin, Round Rock, Georgetown

Interstate 35 travels through downtown Austin and is a major mode of transportation for one of the fastest growing parts of Texas. The capital region is one of the hottest places to move for those in search of new careers working with creative entrepreneurs that produce popular products like YETI and Tito's or the stability of major companies like Dell, Tesla, and Whole Foods. The movement of residents within the region and migration of new residents has transformed the politics of the area, which used to be considered a place that Republican candidates would not dare visit.

The stories of local politics in Austin, as a blue dot in a sea of red, describe the effects of the public sorting itself into communities based on similar ideologies. The lore in thinking of Austin this way is blind to the shifting politics of the surrounding counties that are becoming more like the cultural center. It also underestimates the potential for a Texan candidate to appeal to the Independent voters in Travis County. Understandably, this assumption is reinforced by the historical partisanship of local government institutions in the counties that surround Travis County. That raises an interesting question: Is the increasing support for Democratic candidates occurring at the top of the ticket and down ballot at the same rate?

The major party nominees from Texas in the past thirty years—George H. W. Bush in 1992 and George W. Bush in 2000—received more votes than their Democratic opponents. In 1996 and since 2004, Democratic candidates for president have held double-digit advantages over the Republican candidates, growing as large as 45 percent in 2020. In the same time that Travis County has become more Democratic, the rest of the capital region has too. The less metropolitan counties of Bastrop and Caldwell have steadily supported Republican candidates, as Hays and Williamson counties supported Democratic nominees in 2018 (O'Rourke) and 2020 (Biden) after decades of supporting Republican nominees. It is important to note that in these two growing communities, Governor Abbott ran 13 percent ahead of Senator Ted Cruz on the same ballot in 2018, suggesting that voters in Hays and Williamson counties assess candidate comparisons prior to selecting their preference.

The Republican advantage in the areas outside of Austin is strongest at the local level. Each county in Texas has a County Commissioner's Court made up of four single districts and one county judge elected by the entire county. As of 2020, Bastrop, Caldwell, Hays, and Williamson counties' local decisions were made by Republican-led county governments with three of the four seats being held by Republican nominees. Travis County was the opposite, with Democratic officials holding thee of the four seats. Among the local executives, Hays and Travis counties were led by a Democratic County Judge.

Hays and Williamson counties show the largest signs of how the Greater Austin area is becoming more like Travis County. San Marcos and Round Rock are developing into their own economic centers outside of Austin. The location of the Dell Technologies headquarters in Round Rock is a modern contrast to how the 2020 Democratic nominee for U.S. Senate MJ Hegar introduced herself as growing up in rural Williamson County. At the time she was eighteen years old, the county's population was 172,718 and George W. Bush received 16 percent more of the votes than incumbent Governor Ann Richards. In 2020, when Hegar won the Democratic nomination for U.S. Senate, the county's population was 590,551 and incumbent Senator John Cornyn (R) held a 3 percent margin of victory in that county.

The political change within this region is consequential to the outcome of elections because 9 percent of the state's registered voters reside in the metro area, and in midterm elections the region makes up an even larger share of all votes cast. The above-average turnout in the capital region is in line with observations from other seats of state power, but individually it tracks with the association that individual registered voters in these five counties have higher levels of voter enthusiasm at the time of primary and general elections. Assuming the increased enthusiasm and political knowledge of these voters continues, the Austin area may have greater leverage in future elections as the region attracts new residents with the addition of U.S. Army's Futures Command in downtown Austin and Tesla's Gigafactory in southeast Travis County toward Bastrop County.

San Antonio

San Antonio is Texas's southernmost metropolitan area with more than one million residents. Historically, the area is tied to the state's heritage as a Mexican territory. The community centered around the San Antonio River that rises from the Edwards aquifer is also growing rapidly at this important moment in Texas politics. Census data estimates from 2019 found that San Antonio saw the second largest population increase in the nation.

Partisanship and enthusiasm of voters in San Antonio have varied in the past fourteen years. Voter turnout in the San Antonio area has kept pace with the state average since the 2008 election. From 2018 to 2020, respondents to our surveys indicated that voter enthusiasm was generally comparable between both parties, but 10 percent more Democratic voters indicate they are very enthusiastic than Republican voters in the city.

The variance of party competition in the San Antonio area has cycled based on the office up for election. In the Texas gubernatorial races since 1994, Republican candidates have received the most votes in Bexar County except for 2010 and 2018. The 6 percent that Governor Greg Abbott trailed Sheriff Lupe Valdez in his campaign for reelection is a clear example of how concurrent elections can affect voter enthusiasm. In 2018, Beto O'Rourke received 19 percent more votes than Senator Ted Cruz in Bexar County, which is a major shift from the 12 percent advantage Senator John Cornyn had in the prior Senate race in 2014.

San Antonio is often a priority when the Democratic National Committee is looking to purchase television advertisements. Even though the Biden campaign cancelled most of its $6 million in media purchases across Texas during the first week of early voting, advertisements featuring a Latino veteran continued to air in San Antonio and El Paso to target Latino and Black voters.[7]

Borderlands

The multicultural experience in Texas flows along the Rio Grande River, but its influence in politics is not equivalent in each region along the waterway that separates Texas from Mexico. From El Paso in the northwest to the Rio Grande Valley at the southernmost edge tip of Texas, cultural differences and economic growth shape political attitudes and the partisanship of voters. Engaging voters in these communities has become important to both parties to persuade voters in regions of the state that have lower voter turnout than the rest of the state. Since these are the communities that are majority Latino, the effects of grassroots mobilization are likely to affect local elections and also our measure of Latino voter participation in the aggregate.

The Texas border region has thirty-two counties that lie within 100 miles of the U.S.- Mexico border.[8] Politically, these counties are distinct from one another in ways that outsiders are sure to diminish their credibility if they speak about Texas's borderland as one place using general terms like South Texas, the Rio Grande Valley, or otherwise. We turn first to El Paso; 857 miles west of where I-10 crosses the state's eastern border.

El Paso

El Paso has grown to become a borderplex with its neighboring city Juarez, Mexico. Knowledge about the politics of the era is about as dated as songs and stories from the 1950s that describe it as a special town out in West Texas. The culture of the area is still distinct from the rest of West Texas and the state's border counties, as you would expect for a city that has the Chihuahua Mountains on one side and is isolated from the rest of the state by the Chihuahua Desert.

El Paso is also an important key to the modern political change that is occurring in Texas, because voter turnout in the county is traditionally lower than the state average. This generalization was not true for the 2018 election and voter turnout in El Paso County in 2020 was greater than 50 percent in a presidential election for the first time since 1992. In the twenty-eight years between those two elections the number of registered voters in El Paso County grew by 232 percent, from 210,125 in 1992 to 488,470 registered voters at the time of the 2020 election.

The reengagement of voters in El Paso cannot be untied from the charisma and engagement of Beto O'Rourke's 2018 campaign for the U.S. Senate. When then-city councilman O'Rourke was elected to the U.S. House of Representatives in 2010, only 29 percent of registered voters in El Paso County cast a ballot. El Paso voters began to turn out in larger numbers in the 2014 midterm (40%); voter participation increased another 4 percent in the 2018 election with O'Rourke on the ballot, with 44 percent of registered voters participating in the first election since 2002 when Texans believed a race might be competitive between the two parties.

A comparison of El Paso to its own electoral history tells a story of progress. Voter turnout of registered voters in El Paso County was 9 percent lower than the state average in 2018 and in the 2016 election.[9] As the seventh most populated county in the state of Texas, El Paso is the sleeping giant of Texas politics, particularly if two-party competition is likely to return. The overall turnout in the 2020 election of 54 percent matched the level of voter enthusiasm we found among registered voters who were "very enthusiastic" about voting. That highest level of enthusiasm was 4 percent higher in El Paso County than the state average. Our survey of these voter estimates, 65 percent of registered voters identify or lean to the Democratic Party, which closely matched the vote share that Joe Biden received on November 3, 2020 (67%). The future leverage that votes from El Paso County can have on Texas's elections will come from increasing the number of registered voters who would find ways to get voters who responded that they were "enthusiastic" about voting to participate. The county needs more of those voters, as the response was 6 percent lower than the state average. For these reasons, turnout in El Paso is context dependent and fluctuations can be as large as 1.5 percent of the state's vote share.

Rio Grande Valley

The Rio Grande Valley (RGV) is a compact geographic area along the U.S.-Mexico border surrounding the cities of Brownsville, Edinburg, and McAllen. The entire area includes the counties of Cameron, Hidalgo, Starr, and Willacy. The RGV has a bold and progressive political past harking back to 1967 when farm workers marched four hundred miles from the Rio Grande Valley to Austin to seek a minimum wage of $1.25 an hour.[10] The march was the seed to the creation of La Raza Unida as a political party to elevate the power of the Latino electorate by challenging that the Democratic Party had taken their support for granted. Leaders of the organization looked to broker support for candidates who would expand new economic opportunities in border communities and end school segregation, which would open the door for future social equality.

In the 1960s and 1970s, Lloyd Bentsen, who represented the Rio Grande Valley in the U.S. House before being elected to the Senate, worked to continue a close connection between the Democratic Party and voters of Mexican American descent. The generational replacement of major power brokers in the state, and the emergence of a new generation that is again not satisfied with the status quo, may bring into question how solidly Democratic the region is.

The low point of voter support for the Republican Party in the Rio Grande Valley was the 2016 presidential election, where Donald Trump received 29 percent of the vote from the four-county region after consistently harsh rhetoric and vague statements about Mexican culture and those of Mexican American descent. The exceptional support Democratic candidates receive in the Rio Grande Valley is not limited to the top of the ticket. In 2020, Democratic candidates held all county judge and commissioner positions on the Commissioners' Courts across the four-county region.

The great surprise of the 2020 election was the 13 percent leap in support that Donald Trump received from voters in the Rio Grande Valley after his four years in office, which lived up to the campaign promise of improving and extending the border wall. Despite recently built border wall where preexisting barriers were present and the extension of new border wall to western sections of the RGV, much of the border wall is incomplete.[11] As a recognition of this success, President Trump's last visit to Texas on January 12, 2021, was to speak to residents of Alamo in Hidalgo County about the progress made toward completing the border wall.

The lame-duck visit to Hidalgo County was not President Trump's first visit to the Rio Grande Valley. Two years prior, President Trump visited McAllen on January 10, 2019, amid the government shutdown tied to funding for the border wall.[12] The presidential visit to highlight the work of border patrol agents in the Rio Grande Valley and the continued construction of the wall that followed shifted heightened public awareness to the issue in the region. Among Latinos in the Rio Grande Valley, there was little ambivalence about whether a wall is necessary during this time, with 69 percent of RGV Latinos disagreeing that a wall is necessary versus 29 percent who do. The level of opposition among surveyed Latinos was higher here than in El Paso (49%) where a wall is already present in the community and among Latinos living in the other Borderland counties (26%) that largely do not have a wall on the border. On an issue where prolonged debate often leads to rhetoric that presents Mexico as a problem, we see that 49 percent of Latinos who live 100 miles from the border, away from the major border crossings, are more likely to believe that a wall is necessary for effective border security. Across the Borderlands, attitudes of White voters on the wall differ depending on place, and White voters in El Paso we surveyed are closely divided on the issue (53% agree; 47% disagree).

Electorally, Republicans face less opposition in the Rio Grande Valley and Borderlands than El Paso. In the RGV, the partisan gap in voter identification is 10 percent (49% D; 39% R). The gap widens with Latino voters (55% D; 30% R) but remains close with the state average among registered Latino voters (54% D; 29%). A contributing factor to the Republican lag in the RGV is the partisan identification of White voters who identify as Democrats 10 percent more often than the state average (40% D; 51% R). In the Borderland counties between El Paso and the RGV, any partisan advantage among voter identification is faint (39% D; 37% D) because of the sizable group of voters who do not lean toward either party. These true Independents are the non-White voters of the area, since 59 percent of White voters identify as Republicans and 37 percent identify with the Democratic Party. Thirty-one percent of Latino voters in the Borderlands shy away from identifying as a partisan or leaning to one party (42% D; 27% R).

The ability of Democratic candidates to appeal to voters in the Borderlands with platforms of diversity and inclusion is quelled by an enthusiasm gap between White and Latino voters in the region. Latino voters identify being "very enthusiastic" to vote less often than White voters in the RGV (-12%), El Paso (-7%), and other Borderland counties (-8%). Moreover, 54 percent of White voters in the region supported President Trump across the entire region, which exceeded expectations from partisan identification alone.

The Biden campaign's decision in late October 2020 to send the nominee for vice president, Kamala Harris, during early voting and her husband Doug Emhoff weeks prior reveals that the Democratic Party recognized two lessons from 1970 that were true in 2020. First, votes from the RGV are still key to any victory in the state. Second, the enthusiasm of Latino voters was key to producing a shift in an election outcome. The high-profile candidate visits from national Democratic leaders were a spark but could not overcome the renewal of grassroots efforts by the Republican Party of Texas in 2020.

Discussion and Conclusion

In this chapter we have used interviews and election results to measure the diversity across the state and within seven different regions. Overall, three critical lessons emerged. First, political change in the state is not occurring at the same rate and the shifts we can observe are caused by different factors in each region. Second, outside of the largest cities in the state there is a substantial advantage for one party because of its ability to mobilize voters. Beto O'Rourke's 2018 campaign challenged the conventional wisdom to try to win as many votes in the major cities as possible; he and Julián Castro again pointed to the problem prior to the final week of the 2020 campaign when they demanded that the Biden campaign take Texas seriously and try to increase voter turnout. Finally, it is valuable to pay attention to the local culture as a signal of authenticity but also to strike a balance between new residents and the legacy of the region.

We emphasize the final lesson because the fact that Texas has numerous large urban areas, each with its own identity, means there is not a risk-averse way to appeal to the electorate. For candidates who fail to execute an attempt to enjoy Texas's flavor, the consequences can be damning. Few examples are as notable as when President Gerald Ford bit into a tamale, still wrapped in its husk, at a San Antonio restaurant in April of 1976. The public mistake became known as the "Great Tamale Incident," even though it is unlikely related to Jimmy Carter's victory in Texas, which is now historical because a Democratic candidate for president has not won the state of Texas since.

Learning these lessons and navigating Texas's unique political culture is more difficult for national candidates. The heavy concentration of registered voters in Houston, San Antonio, Dallas–Fort Worth, and Austin is a clear attraction for candidates to frequently visit the largest metropolitan areas, the medium cities less, and small cities when possible. Today when we see candidates visit these large cities, we must understand that the setting is a selection of convenience and while there may be fewer Republican voters in the central city those candidates need to maintain the enthusiasm of voters in the neighboring counties.

The realization that the 2020 presidential election in Texas was decided by the percentage of voters that President Trump won in small towns and rural communities is something with which both parties must contend. Texas Republicans must recognize the instability of how population growth, primarily in the urban areas, has continued to alter the party's coalition of being competitive in the largest metro areas and dominating politics in small towns and rural areas of the state. Rural Texas has produced a smaller portion of votes in each election since 1992. For Texas Democrats, survey research over three years has shown that the estimated partisan breakdown of rural voters is closer than metropolitan areas with less than 250,000 residents that are mostly in East Texas. Inroads at any level, or partial adjustments in all of Texas's regions must be a goal of the larger party organizations.

CHAPTER 4

The Reemergence of Texas Democrats
on the National Stage

Those 38 Electoral College votes in Texas are now in play, and I can win them.
—Beto O'Rourke, 2019[1]

FOLLOWING THE REAGAN REVOLUTION, which flipped many Southern states to vote for a Republican nominee for president for decades, Bill Clinton has been the only Democratic president from the South. Are Democratic candidates from the South still able to energize their state and reach a national audience? To answer this, we look at how Texas voters evaluated two Texans who ran for the Democratic nomination for president in 2020. Neither Beto O'Rourke nor Julián Castro won the Texas Democratic Primary, but voters in the state were offered a choice they had not had since 1988.

Since 2000, every Democratic nominee for president has come from a state that previously voted for a Republican in 1988 (Delaware, Illinois, and Tennessee) or 1984 (Massachusetts and New York). During the 2008 election, Obama flipped Florida, North Carolina, and Virginia. In 2012, he only won Virginia again. Obama's victories were motivated not by his familiarity with the electorate, but his ability to connect with voters in states with significant demographic changes from new residents.[2] Biden's 2020 victory in Georgia has been described in a similar vein.[3] We should not forget that Clinton, Gore, Obama, and Biden also found ways to make even more Southern states competitive, extending the metaphor that Democrats could win in a loss by beating expectations.

Expectations from demographic changes renewed the ambition of two Texans to seek the Democratic nomination in 2020. These were also the only two candidates in the primary from a Southern state. Former secretary of Housing and Urban Development and former mayor of San Antonio, Julián Castro, announced his candidacy on January 12, 2019. Former U.S. Representative Beto O'Rourke (D-TX) from El Paso followed with his own announcement two months later. If either were to win the nomination it would be a chance to see if a Democratic nominee could reestablish the magic that Bill Clinton created in Texas when the state was last considered to be a battleground state. Clinton came within 4 percent of George H. W. Bush during the 1992 election and 5 percent of Bob Dole in 1996. In both elections, Clinton was aided by having Ross Perot on the ballot as an alternative who advocated for less government intervention.[4]

Castro and O'Rourke were both considered dark horses to win the nomination in 2020. The twenty-nine-candidate field was crowded, but the two Texans worked to distinguish themselves from the rest of the field. Castro was the only Latino candidate. O'Rourke was bolstered by a youthful persona and name recognition as the only candidate in the race who had come close to winning a large Southern state. Both candidates set themselves apart from Donald Trump on issues that were local to Texans, including immigration, border security, and gun control. They believed they were the best option for a Democrat to beat President Trump by winning Texas. The promise of winning Texas's Democratic primary also presented a narrow path for a candidate with low name recognition in other regions to amass a large delegate count on Super Tuesday.

The emergence of two Texans for the Democratic nomination for president presented a new opportunity to see if Texas Democrats would be engaged in the early stages of the primary process. Would voters exhibit more support for the home state candidates? Would voters change their opinions as they became more familiar with other candidates? By taking a chance to run for national office Julián Castro and Beto O'Rourke elevated the impact Texas could have in the Democratic Party and provided two opportunities for the national party to engage Latino voters in a new way. The allure of being able to compete in California and Texas where Latino voters outnumber Black voters set the option for a new campaign for candidates who had less support in Iowa and New Hampshire. The Texas primary also offered a new opportunity because of a rule change in 2015 that provides an advantage to candidates who attract double-digit support in the state. Texas's Democratic delegates are now pledged to a candidate if they receive 15 percent or more of

Table 4.1. Chronology of the Texas Democratic Party on Super Tuesday

Year	Winner	Primary Vote	Date
2020	Joe Biden	35	March 3
2016	Hillary Clinton	65	March 1
2008	Hillary Clinton	60	March 4
2004	John Kerry	67	March 9
2000	Al Gore	80	March 14
1992	Bill Clinton	66	March 10
1988	Michael Dukakis	33	March 8
1984	Walter Mondale	52	May 5
1976	Jimmy Carter	47	May 1

In 2012, the Texas Democratic Party held a convention to determine how to distribute their delegates.

the vote or win a state senate district. The straightforward process replaced the Texas two-step that included a primary and caucus on the night of the election.

Stopping the Two-Step Gave People the Power

As table 4.1 illustrates, Texas began to hold its presidential primary on Super Tuesday in 1988, twelve years after the multistate primary day was created by other Southern states to help Governor Jimmy Carter (D-GA).[5] Even as an early, delegate-rich state, the Texas Democratic Primary did not attract national attention because the winning candidate was not assured he would receive the most delegates. A two-step process involving a primary and a caucus was used between 1976 and 2012, allowing delegates to be split as they were in 1988 when Michael Dukakis won the Texas Democratic Primary and Jesse Jackson won the Texas Democratic Caucus. By allowing the general public to determine who receives Texas's delegates, there are fewer opportunities for delegates to be pledged to candidates Texas Democrats do not support, like when George Wallace won delegates from the Texas Democratic Convention.[6]

The rule change went largely unnoticed in 2016 because Texas voters in the Democratic Primary were expected to support the frontrunner again. Former Senator and Secretary of State Hillary Clinton (D-NY) won the 2016 Texas Democratic Primary over Senator Bernie Sanders (I-VT) with 65 percent of the vote. The 2020 primary posed a much different context. The crowded primary with candidates who had direct Texas ties increased with Texans in the race and a large field of twenty-nine candidates and improved the likelihood that Texas voters would remain engaged. The expectation of a prolonged nomination battle also increased the value of winning the largest share of Texas's delegates.

Challenge of Name Recognition in a Large Field of Candidates

The rush of candidates announcing their candidacy for president was a response to the Democratic National Committee's announcement in December 2018 that the first televised debate of primary candidates would occur in June of 2019. Candidates were told that debate qualifications would be decided based on the candidate's popularity in polls and levels of grassroots fundraising, which further accelerated the need to quickly establish a campaign.

The first of these candidates to announce was Senator Elizabeth Warren (D-MA), quickly followed by Representative Tulsi Gabbard (D-HI), and Julián Castro past Mayor of San Antonio.[7] Julián Castro's entrance into the race was the first time a Texan sought the Democratic nomination for president since Senator Lloyd Bentsen (D-TX) lost his race for the 1976 nomination to Governor Jimmy Carter (D-GA). The field continued to grow as Senator Cory Booker (D-NJ), Senator Amy Klobuchar (D-MN), and former U.S. Representative Beto O'Rourke announced their candidacies in early February.

Within a week of O'Rourke's announcement, we conducted a statewide poll of 1,049 registered voters in Texas, including 348 likely Democratic Primary voters. We asked potential Democratic primary voters which candidate they would support from a list of candidates who received the most media coverage since entering the 2020 primary election. The responses from the voters clearly showed that three months after the 2018 Senate election in Texas, Democrats continued to believe in O'Rourke as a candidate. O'Rourke held the strongest support of voters across the state (47%) in this early poll, indicating a strong advantage over fellow Texan Julián Castro as well as nationally known candidates Senator Elizabeth Warren (D-MA) and Senator Kamala Harris (D-CA). The gap between O'Rourke and all other candidates signals the clear name recognition and high expectations his campaign began with.

Table 4.2. Candidate Support among Texas Voters, February 2019

Candidate	Support	Duration of Campaign
Beto O'Rourke (D-TX)	47%	5 days
Kamala Harris (D-CA)	7	20 days
Elizabeth Warren (D-MA)	6	41 days
Julián Castro (D-TX)	5	29 days
Amy Klobuchar (D-MN)	2	1 day
Cory Booker (D-NJ)	2	10 days
Kirsten Gillibrand (D-NY)	1	26 days
Other or Undecided	31	
	n = 348	

Beto O'Rourke's strong connection with Texas Democrats grew after he sparked national discussions as a potential new face for the Democratic Party and raised $6.1 million in one day. He showed he would aggressively campaign against President Donald Trump by officially announcing his candidacy on the day President Trump was in O'Rourke's hometown, El Paso, for a rally in March to promote building a border wall along the Mexico border. This provided O'Rourke with an immediate opportunity to contrast himself to the incumbent president and emphasize the importance he saw in an integrated society at the border.

The real test for Texas's native son would be how would this popularity continue once frontrunner candidates like Senator Bernie Sanders (I-VT) and former Vice President Joe Biden would enter the race. In the absence of an active campaign, the effect of O'Rourke's name recognition attracted support from all demographics. More than a quarter of the Independent candidates had a clear preference and they comprised 10 percent of O'Rourke's statewide support. O'Rourke was preferred by 57 percent of Latino voters, which comprised 11 percent of his support.

The first candidate debate stood as a test for whether Joe Biden and Bernie Sanders would overwhelm the large field of candidates with their name recognition from previously running for president. If Biden and Sanders were unable to become the frontrunners in Texas, then the debates could cause a shift in support in two ways. The debates would allow candidates with less name recognition to consolidate support by taking votes away from the leading candidates among Texas voters (Biden, O'Rourke, and Sanders); this is known as a *narrowing effect*. If a Texan were to remain atop the large field of candidates there would be evidence to suggest Texas Democrats support a candidate who would appear as a localized effect.

A narrowing effect is an example of a phenomenon that seems to recur no matter who the candidates are in an election.[8] Narrowing occurs when the leader of early polls either loses or wins by a smaller margin than the early polls would indicate. Under this theory, the polls respond to election events throughout the campaign cycle, to incumbency, or the state of the economy. The larger point is that there is a "stable context" within which campaigns operate and the early leader before the campaign begins is not likely to maintain a large lead in the polls as the respective campaigns unfold.[9] Narrowing occurs more or less automatically over time as the early leader's advantage becomes smaller and smaller as the net effects of campaign events, emergence of new candidates, and uncontrollable events (such as changes in the economy or foreign policy problems) impact the polls. We explore whether Texas primary voters have a local preference for a national nominee, which could allow a Texan to catapult themselves to the national discussion.

Candidate Exposure and Momentum from the June Debate

The early popularity of native-Texan Beto O'Rourke among Texas voters in 2019 was an extension from the positive name recognition he developed in the 2018 campaign. This also made him the leader among Texas voters who would be subject to the narrowing effect once voters had the opportunity to compare him side by side with other national candidates during the televised Democratic debates. Nationally, Joe Biden and Bernie Sanders were the most well-known candidates, and they were the last to announce their candidacies. Texans would have to wait months before O'Rourke would be on stage with all the frontrunner candidates due to the logistics of hosting a televised debate for twenty candidates who received some support in national polls or had displayed enough fundraising success to meet the standard set by the Democratic Party for an invitation.

In the first split-stage debate, O'Rourke and Castro were both assigned to the first night. The center of the stage focused attention on Warren and O'Rourke because they had the strongest support among voters among the ten candidates randomly assigned to the event. Biden, Sanders, Pete Buttigieg, and Kamala Harris were assigned to the second night of the debate and the two center podiums were occupied by Biden and Sanders. We followed both events with another poll of Texas voters to provide a comprehensive look at who the voters supported now that almost all the candidates had joined the race to participate in the debate.

The first split-stage Democratic debate generated different storylines by declaring two different winners of the debate. In the first night, Senator Warren quickly showed that she could demand the public's attention and was the most formidable debater in the field. Following her debate performance, she increased her support by 4 percent among Texas voters. Warren's support was highest among those who watched some part of the debate (17%) and those who watched all the debate (13%). These points suggest that the first debate provided Harris and Warren with an opportunity to build early momentum. Interestingly, we found among Texas voters who watched all the debate in Miami, support for Harris was higher (+9%). Senator Harris generated 3 percent more support from debate watchers than her overall support with the electorate. The increase in voter support for these candidates, while others remained stagnant, indicates simply being in the debate was not enough to establish a narrowing effect early in the election.

The ability of two candidates to generate momentum suggests that the effect of the debate was not equal, even though the assignment of candidates to each evening was random. The requirement of voters to tune in to a two-hour broadcast on consecutive nights was particularly high. Among our survey of Democratic voters who watched any portion of the first two-night Democratic presidential debate, only 31 percent of voters watched the debate on both nights. The fact that only one-third of the debate watchers tuned in for both nights indicates that voters themselves presented a new selection effect that truncated the potential for candidates to generate momentum from a strong debate performance.

After the debate, much of the media's attention focused on the second debate, particularly Senator Kamala Harris's critique of former Vice President Joe Biden's voting record on civil rights early in his career as a senator. By challenging the frontrunner on stage, Harris attracted the public's attention and established that the public's memory of the debate would be about Biden versus Harris. The positive press that Harris received by emerging as a contender from the first debate appeared in the polls to be enough to maintain the public support she previously had with seven percent in Texas.

Table 4.3. Candidate Support after the First Two-Night Debate, July 2019

Candidate	Support	Debate Night
Beto O'Rourke	26%	1
Joe Biden	23	2
Bernie Sanders	17	2
Elizabeth Warren	10	1
Kamala Harris	7	2
Pete Buttigieg	4	2
Julián Castro	4	1
Cory Booker	2	1
Michael Bennett	2	2

Note: Candidates Steve Bullock, John Hickenlooper, Amy Klobuchar, Joe Sestak, Tom Steyer, and Marian Williamson each received 1 percent in the poll. Other candidates, including Kirsten Gillibrand, Bill De Blasio, John Delaney, Tulsi Gabbard, Jay Inslee, Wayne Messam, Seth Moulton, Tim Ryan, and Andrew Yang, did not receive more than 0.5 percent in a survey of 324 Texas Democrats and Independents that lean Democratic (MOE +/- 3.4%).

Separating the field of candidates into two contests eliminated the ability of voters to measure candidates side by side. It also increased the cost of voters to be exposed to all candidates by requiring voters to watch six total hours of debates over two nights. Both factors support the logic that one split-debate could be a primary predictor to narrow voter support for the candidates. As more candidates entered the race, O'Rourke's own numbers predictably declined among voters in the state. The changes in which candidate was the top choice remained tied to which candidate was preferred by Independents that leaned to the Democratic Party and by Hispanic voters. In that case we turn to our survey of voters in July 2019, which occurred between the first and second Democratic presidential debates.

The results of the July poll (table 4.3) show that O'Rourke maintained his support among Texas voters five months into the election. The reports in Texas suggesting O'Rourke did not meet expectations in the debate should have signaled momentum for another candidate. O'Rourke remained the strong favorite among Independents and Hispanic voters in Texas. The early enthusiasm for O'Rourke that seemed to be dampened was simply a shift of voter support to the new candidates who entered after he did with former

Vice President Joe Biden and Senator Bernie Sanders both securing double-digit support.

The persistence of the strong and favorable evaluation of O'Rourke among Texas voters was more impressive as national candidates turned their attention to Texas with respect to policy. One of the most prominent policy debates was how far each candidate would go to oppose the family separation policy of the Trump administration at immigration facilities, particularly those along the U.S.-Mexico border. The combination of an increasing field of candidates and the localized attention national candidates sought to offer for Texas voters suggests O'Rourke influenced the narrative of the campaign. This signifies the value of additional study about how debate effects influence the early stages of a campaign in specific states.

Narrowing Effect from the Second Debate: A Panel Study of Texas Voters

After the Miami debate, the Democratic Party was set to host another debate at the end of July in Detroit. This meant it would be possible to differentiate between momentum and a narrowing effect by observing voter opinions across multiple debates.[10] We re-interviewed the respondents from our July poll after the Detroit debate to see if candidates were developing a relative advantage over one another with Texas voters.[11]

By tracking the opinions of Texas voters before and after the debates on July 30 and 31, 2019, we were able to determine that the Democratic debate generated two separate and independent debate effects. The narrowing effect between candidates who participated on the same debate stage was larger. Also, the momentum candidates gained appeared to be at the expense of candidates who participated in the second night of the debate. This is an effect likely associated with voters selectively watching candidates on one but not both nights. Candidates randomly assigned to the second night received less momentum because there was greater interest in watching a debate where Sanders, Warren, Buttigieg, and O'Rourke were at the center of the stage.

During the second Democratic debate, both Warren and Sanders commanded more time than any other candidate. This was clearly driven by a longer exchange that was allowed for a policy debate over healthcare alternatives. In addition to speaking the most about healthcare, Warren also spoke the longest about foreign policy and immigration. By being kept out of the policy discussions, Warren and Sanders narrowed the relative advantage O'Rourke held over the two senators in the eyes of the Texas voters. This resulted in Warren improving her appeal with college-educated female voters by 10 percent. In this contrast, O'Rourke was the only candidate who lost support among females with a bachelor's degree following this debate as other women shifted their support to Biden (+15%) and Buttigieg (+6%).

An artifact of the split debate was the appearance that Biden developed momentum, especially since he become the favored candidate in Texas after the second debate. Biden was the only candidate in the second night of the debate who started with double-digit support among Texas voters. To Biden's benefit, the relative advantage he had over other candidates on the stage during the second night allowed him to speak more than any other candidate during the two nights. The additional debate time and attention dedicated to discussions of civil rights in the second night also offered a different context for voters to frame their comparison of the candidates. As Senators Booker and Harris challenged Biden to clarify his previous voting record on civil rights, he was able to further align himself with President Obama. This allowed Biden to maintain his support among the Black voters who identified with the Democratic Party or leaned toward the party. Biden's ability to pivot to the broader goals of economic fairness allowed him to appeal to 5 percent more Latino voters. With all eyes on Biden, it was difficult for other candidates to generate momentum from the second night. We also see that the momentum that Harris generated from a similar critique of the vice president in the first debate evaporated after the second debate.

Interestingly, the actions of candidates to contrast themselves against Biden in the second night did not change the preferences of voters in Texas the way it did when voters were able to compare candidates to O'Rourke. The contrasts between each night of the second debate are evidence that more can be gained by understanding if there was greater variation in voter support for candidates among specific coalitions. Some reasons for this become apparent as we delve deeper into the numbers.

Our ability to follow up with voters after the debate revealed that voters in Texas were shifting their support as they learned new information about the candidates. Between the two polls, there were few national events that drew more attention to the campaign than the debates. In our survey, 13 percent of voters admitted the debate changed their mind about which candidate to support. Ten percent of potential Democratic primary voters also admitted

Table 4.4. Candidate Preference among Texas Voters, August 2019

Candidate	Pre-Debate	Post-Debate	Change	Speaking Time	Night
Joe Biden	23%	28%	+5%	22 minutes	2
Beto O'Rourke	26	19	-7	11	1
Bernie Sanders	17	18	+1	18	1
Elizabeth Warren	10	13	+3	19	1
Kamala Harris	7	4	-3	17	2
Julián Castro	4	4	—	11	2
Pete Buttigieg	4	4	—	14	1
Cory Booker	2	3	+1	13	2
Michael Bennett	2	1	-1	11	2
Marianne Williamson	1	1	—	9	1
Tulsi Gabbard	0	1	+1	11	2
Andrew Yang	0	1	+1	9	2
Amy Klobuchar	1	0	-1	11	1
Steve Bullock	1	0	-1	11	1
John Hickenlooper	1	0	-1	9	1
Kirsten Gillibrand	0	0	—	12	2
Tim Ryan	0	0	—	10	1
Jay Inslee	0	0	—	11	2
John Delaney	0	0	—	11	1
Bill De Blasio	0	0	—	9	2

that the post-debate analyses also shaped the opinion of the candidates. Our goal of interviewing voters twice was to see from where candidates were gaining support. Figure 4.1 illustrates the support lost by one candidate to another, with wider bands representing more voters and each band connecting the candidate a voter initially supported with the candidate they supported after the debate.

Because the Texas primary is a semi-open primary where voters publicly state to election officials the party primary in which they wish to vote, is important to track the views of Democrats and Independents that lean Democratic. A comparison of voter opinions from the pre-debate and post-debate polls show, with respect to partisanship, the narrowing effect of the second

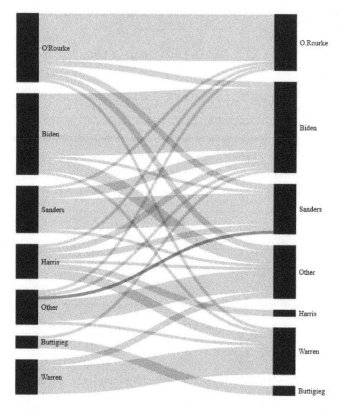

Figure 4.1: Voter Shifts after the Second Debate

Democratic primary debate was most prominent among Independent voters. Any candidate who could transform the electorate in this way would need to have large and clear support from Independent voters. Interestingly, our pre-debate poll showed Independent voters who leaned to the Democratic Party were not immediately attracted to outsiders as seen by the 62 percent advantage O'Rourke had over Sanders in July. After the second debate Independent voters that leaned to the Democratic Party in Texas shifted to support either Biden (22% increase) or Sanders (20% increase). While the swing among Independents clearly came at the expense of voter support for O'Rourke, it is a common trend associated with narrowing and the increasing exposure other candidates gain from the debate stage. Also, the stability of candidate preferences among voters who identified with the Democratic Party following an event that produced large shifts in the preferences of Independents that lean to the Democratic Party shows a difference in how quickly each type of voter is to commit to a candidate.

Following the negative evaluations of O'Rourke's debate performance by media outlets in Texas, the magnitude of the O'Rourke coalition switching to favor another candidate suggests a strong narrowing effect for Independents because his support declined in two successive polls. The context of the split debate made it difficult for candidates who needed momentum to find it. Among Texas voters who did not identify as Democrats, but leaned toward the party, their support shifted only among the three candidates with the highest name recognition among Texas voters early in the contest. Moreover, the shifts in support for Biden and Sanders were almost equal, casting doubt on a suggestion that either candidate truly gained momentum with the constituency. The last source of strong evidence that the early shift in the polls was primarily a narrowing effect was O'Rourke's ability to maintain his slight advantage among self-identified Democrats over Biden (+2) and a larger lead over Sanders (+9). In this reflection, partisans serve as a valuable control group for this comparison because they often know more about the policy views of national party members that would be used by candidates to introduce themselves in these debates.

All Candidates on the Texas Stage

Both Texas candidates maintained their positions in the top half of the field for the Democratic nomination. The following debate in Houston on ABC News and Telemundo ended the national Democratic Party's process of randomly assigning candidates to different nights of a debate. One debate would feature the top ten candidates on September 12, 2019. The combination of Houston as the host city and allowing all candidates to be on the stage at the same time created an opportunity for candidates to build momentum by talking about issues that were important in Texas. In the first two debates Biden and O'Rourke had not been on the same stage together and neither had Castro or Sanders.

The timing of the debate was important for the two native son candidates Castro and O'Rourke, both of whom were trailing nationally and both staking their candidacy on performing well in Texas. In many ways both candidates were right to believe in their ability to appeal to Texas voters, but they were also both direct rivals for that constituency. Castro and O'Rourke led

all Democratic candidates in the number of donations and total dollars do-
nated by Texans among all Democratic candidates. Between January 1 and
September 30, O'Rourke raised $5.9 million from Texas donors with many of
those donors coming from small donations. During the same period, Castro
received the third most donations from Texans with $1.1 million, which was
$300,000 less than Sanders.[12] Despite the favored status of both Castro and
O'Rourke among Texas voters, their popularity was not the same in other
areas of the nation. Playing to the advantage they had, both campaigns tried
to sell themselves nationally by keeping the faith of supporters in the state to
claim Texas's delegates.

Both Castro and O'Rourke would have to fight for attention in this debate
because they were sidelined to the end of the debate stage next to each other.
That attention would be hard to find, because fourteen million viewers across
the nation were likely attracted to compare Senator Warren to former Vice
President Biden as they shared the same debate stage for the first time. Moreover, the Texans would have to find ways to pivot to their issue platforms
because events prior to the debate relating to a mass shooting at an El Paso
Walmart on August 3, 2019, would predictably be the first question asked to
candidates in their home state. There were twenty-two victims of the terrible
act of violence, and the shooter's motivation was to target Latinos. Weeks before this had affected the campaign when O'Rourke left the campaign trail to
be with residents of his hometown and he then focused much of his attention
on elevating discussions about how to advance policies to promote gun safety.
The renewed attention to his campaign was also starting to build back toward
the initial high expectations with which his campaign started.

The moderators of the debate specifically provided O'Rourke time to
speak directly about gun safety, presenting him with an unusual opportunity
to start a policy discussion on stage. O'Rourke showed empathy as a leader
and accepted empathy from the other candidates before pivoting to promote
solutions to stop gun violence. During the debate David Muir asked a clari-
fying question: "Are you proposing taking away their guns? And how would
this work?" A memorable moment was O'Rourke's passionate answer, "Hell
yes, we're going to take your AR-15, your AK-47. We're not going to allow it
to be used against our fellow Americans anymore."[13]

The other candidates followed down the line with their own reflections. A
clear contrast was the competitiveness between the candidates that emerged
in the third debate, which began at this moment. The candidates leading

O'Rourke in the polls continued to show empathy to the people of El Paso, but the candidates who saw a resurgent O'Rourke as a challenge to their own candidacy offered sharp criticism of the former representative. Senator Kamala Harris said "Beto, God love you for standing so courageously in the middle of that tragedy," before she offered to take executive action to make it more difficult to purchase guns. Senator Cory Booker suggested that O'Rourke only cared about the issue once a mass-shooting occurred in his hometown. Former Mayor Pete Buttigieg also claimed O'Rourke was being too radical by advocating for policy issues that would face opposition instead of passing legislation that had more support.

Following this debate, we randomly polled registered voters in Texas a third time to have a fresh sample and new perspective of the race after our short panel study surrounding the second debate. Even if the former Rhodes scholars Booker and Buttigieg were not swayed by O'Rourke's call to action, Texans were. Despite low national approval, O'Rourke remained one of the top two candidates among potential voters in the Texas Democratic primary. Also, when we asked which candidate voters trusted about gun policy, the Democratic voters trusted O'Rourke by a large margin after he elevated the conversation about reducing the number of automatic weapons. Locally, a mass shooting is an uncontrollable event that can shape public opinion when leaders are willing to publicly debate solutions.

Our poll also showed that the third debate was Biden's first source of real momentum with Texas voters. In the previous three months Biden's coalition grew at a similar rate to the growing appeal for Sanders as O'Rourke's lead narrowed. After comparing O'Rourke and Biden on the same stage with the eight other top candidates, Biden's lead grew, and O'Rourke and Sanders remained steady. This debate in Houston was when Biden was able to attract more support (31%) from Texas's Black voters than O'Rourke (25%). The increasing credit claiming by Biden for his role in achieving the results of the Obama administration likely helped with this. For example, voters who wanted a nominee that would protect President Obama's legacy supported O'Rourke (22%) and Biden (21%) over other candidates, adding to Biden's growing support. By promoting his direct connection with the Obama administration, Biden provided a contrast with his experience and O'Rourke's optimistic views that was intended to attract voters.

We may look back on this debate and remember Beto's love of El Paso or Biden's quip to characterize Sanders as a socialist, but each anecdote likely did more to keep a coalition together instead of attracting new votes. Our three consecutive surveys showed the extended debate process that took place in the invisible primary connected with groups of Texas voters at different times. Or perhaps more interesting, groups of Texas voters changed their candidate preferences at different moments as new information became available and contrasts between candidates became clearer. The absence of a clear front-runner in Texas this early also revealed the diversity of candidate preferences within the Texas electorate for Democrats. Many saw O'Rourke as a contender to Biden, especially as both O'Rourke and Biden received positive evaluations from 22 percent of those who watched the third debate. Also, having three equally competitive candidates among Latino Democrats—Biden 24 percent, O'Rourke 22 percent, and Sanders 22 percent—revealed that without a cue for incumbency the Latino electorate in the Democratic Party has diverse preferences.

Discussion and Conclusion

These shifts in candidate preference are important to understand the complexity of Texas's electorate. Throughout the campaign, Texas voters largely considered three candidates and each of them provided a different appeal within Texas's triethnic electorate. The coalition of voters who supported former Vice President Biden early on were self-identified partisans, African Americans, and individuals who wanted to continue President Obama's legacy. Conversely, Senator Sanders grew his popularity by appealing to Independent voters who leaned to the Democratic Party, Latino voters, and individuals who wanted a candidate who would energize the base. The candidate who truly defined the invisible primary was Beto O'Rourke who held significant support across each voter demographic and voters who wanted to continue President Obama's legacy and those voters who wanted to support a candidate who held the same policies as they did.

The subtle shifts in candidate support among each voter coalition suggest that in the 2020 Texas Democratic primary, the debate provided a narrowing effect to benefit former Vice President Biden and Senator Sanders. During the invisible primary that began on December 31, 2018, we see that most Texas voters supported either of the two national frontrunners or the native son that had run statewide. This trend becomes even more important when the election continued after both O'Rourke and Castro suspended their campaigns after not qualifying for the October and November debates.

The eventual momentum that Biden and Sanders were able to manufacture within the Texas electorate only came when O'Rourke dropped out of the race. This would seem ironic since it was the announcement of the Biden and Sanders candidacies that rivaled O'Rourke's support across the state that fueled his confidence while campaigning nationally. The one constant for all three of these candidates is that they were able to attract more than 15 percent within each large voter group within the Texas electorate.

CHAPTER 5

Primaries and WhataBiden!
on Super Tuesday

There is no statewide constituency in Texas for a moderate Republican.
—Paul Burka, 2018[1]

WINNING THE REPUBLICAN NOMINATION has become the most valuable prize in statewide elections. Aside from long-time incumbents, moderate Republicans have found it increasingly difficult to win the early elections. The division within the party preceded the election of Donald Trump, but the role of populist ideals to shake up political consensus is quite similar, especially at the primary stage.

The rules that govern these party primaries in Texas matter because they allow any registered voter to participate in a general election and later in a run-off election. In Texas the freedom to vote in any election has not encouraged more turnout in primary elections. In 2020, 25 percent of all registered voters cast a ballot on Super Tuesday. Texas's recent highwater mark for voter turnout in primary elections was 30 percent in 2008. Since each primary election is a contest between different candidates in an independent context, let's look at a few cases that capture how the nomination process in Texas is changing.

Paul Burka's reflection in *Texas Monthly* that "[t]here is no statewide constituency in Texas for a moderate Republican" was a direct comment on the career of Lieutenant Governor David Dewhurst. Dewhurst started in Texas politics in 1998 when he was elected as commissioner of the General Land Office. After completing one term, Dewhurst, who was known for being exceptionally tall and rather wealthy, revealed that he was also a strategic politician who would only run for the party nomination once the incumbent was no longer in office.

Once Governor George W. Bush was inaugurated as president of the United States in January of 2001, it was clear there would be a lot of interest in state elections in the upcoming election. Dewhurst announced his intention to run for lieutenant governor early during the legislative session, which accelerated the decision of Lieutenant Governor Bill Ratliff, who had planned to run after being elected by the Texas Senate to fill the term of Rick Perry. Ratliff announced his candidacy at the end of the legislative session in 2001 but abruptly ended the campaign ten days later. Ratliff was uncomfortable with running an election that could cost $10 million. The reason this was a real possibility was because Dewhurst was wealthy enough to fund his own campaign. At the same time, other major contenders like Greg Abbott opted to run for attorney general rather than challenge Dewhurst.

After David Dewhurst defeated former Comptroller John Sharp with 52 percent of the vote in 2020, he was reelected in 2006 with 56 percent of the vote and 62 percent of the vote in 2010. As he continued to wait for the next opportunity, Senator Kay Bailey Hutchison announced she would not seek reelection in 2012. Dewhurst immediately emerged as the frontrunner in the Senate race because he was favored by the Republican establishment. After finishing first in the primary, Dewhurst lost the primary run-off election to then Solicitor General Ted Cruz by 14 percent (57% to 43%). Cruz received enthusiastic support from the Tea Party, including endorsements from populist Republicans like Sarah Palin and Rick Santorum.

Time and staggered elections can heal some wounds from past elections, but for Dewhurst the 2014 Republican primary for lieutenant governor proved this was not the case. The 2012 primary run-off election showed there was an active constituency who would oppose the long-time incumbent, especially if he was perceived to be a moderate. Land Commissioner Jerry Patterson, Agriculture Commissioner Todd Staples, and State Senator Dan Patrick all crowded Dewhurst's primary. Dewhurst (28%) and Patrick (41%) moved on to the May party primary run-off election, at which point Patrick defeated Dewhurst by 30 percent (65% to 35%). The grassroots support for Patrick appears to have been larger than that of Cruz, even though turnout in the party run-off fell by 3 percent to 5.5 percent of all registered voters when we compare participation to the 2012 Republican primary run-off for the Senate.

The electoral defeats of David Dewhurst present an example of how a business-friendly Republican can attract 60 percent of the vote in a general election but fail to earn the party nomination when turnout continues to decline. Since the 2012 election, Republican candidates for statewide office have been weary of falling to the left of the primary electorate. As a result, centrist Republicans and ambitious Democratic candidates have strategically decided to serve regions of the state until the power of the Republican label diminishes, or centrist voters return to vote in primary elections.

Trying to pick the winner of a nomination before the voters cast their ballots is an exceptionally difficult task. Early in the campaign sources of candidate strength such as name recognition, campaign war chests, and voter enthusiasm vary between candidates and are unique to each election. Historically, primary elections have always had less turnout than the general elections and run-off elections have even less. Furthermore, the rules of the primary election split the electorate by forcing voters to select one party's ballot.

Voter turnout is affected by the context of these elections.[2] Primary voting can appear less consequential because each party has a winner, and the candidates simply moves on to the next round. Voters are most likely to participate in primary elections when an election for president, senator, or governor is on the ballot. When the elections are hotly contested, the probability of increasing turnout is also higher. That logic does not always extend to run-off elections for two reasons that depress turnout. The election is held two months after the primary, but only for the offices in which a candidate did not receive 50 percent of the vote. Voters are traditionally less likely to return for two very different reasons. They either find both remaining candidates acceptable or voters may not be enthusiastic to vote because their favored candidate is no longer on the ballot. As voters lose interest in participating in more than one election, the opportunities for surprise outcomes increase because candidates with small but committed constituencies can hit the margin needed to continue to the next stage and possibly pick up the nomination.

WhataBiden

As Texas's primaries have become more treacherous for moderate Republicans, Texas Democrats have been supportive of centrist Democrats in statewide elections. The difference between the preferences of both primary electorates is driven by the context of who holds political power in the state. Democrats have been more likely to support candidates with high name recognition, bipartisan pasts, or charismatic leaders because the priority is to win an election. Republicans expect that the electorate will continue to support they party's nominees so battles between candidates are about ideology and style.

National Democrats have traditionally relied on endorsements from elected officials in Texas to develop an image of being electable. Joe Biden's campaign overperformed on Super Tuesday, not because of a grassroots organization, but because of a concerted effort by influential Democratic officials in Texas to support the former vice president. Ten high profile Democratic elected officials endorsed Biden prior to the election, including eight of Texas's twelve Democratic U.S. representatives, Austin's mayor Steve Adler, and former Dallas mayor Mike Rawlings. Endorsements for other candidates were limited to Elizabeth Warren who was endorsed by Joaquin and Julián Castro, Representative Al Green's endorsement of Kamala Harris, and Houston's mayor Sylvester Turner's late endorsement of Mike Bloomberg. Once early voting began, one major political voice in Texas had not yet announced his endorsement.

The darling of the Texas Democratic Party, Beto O'Rourke, had not signaled which former rival for the Democratic nomination he would endorse. Instead, he worked with Powered by the People to energize volunteers to try to support candidates for the state legislature. With the nation's attention squarely on Texas and Super Tuesday, O'Rourke used a political rally in Dallas on the eve of the election to jump on stage with Senator Amy Klobuchar and announce that they would both endorse Joe Biden.

The timing of the endorsement felt like an emergency reset button on the campaign, which ended Biden's slide in the Lonestar state by reestablishing a focus on the candidate characteristics that made him the frontrunner in Texas. Moreover, the moment occurred one week after U.S. House Majority Whip James Clyburn's powerful endorsement in South Carolina breathed new life into Biden's struggling campaign by saying, "We know Joe. But more importantly, he knows us."[3]

Sanders's Surge and Biden's Recovery

While Joe Biden banked on a boost in the delegate count by winning most of Texas's delegates, other candidates had high levels of name recognition and had developed a sense of electability. Support for Bernie Sanders began to escalate in February after delayed election results in Iowa signaled that Sanders shared the lead in Iowa and he won New Hampshire. Within three days of winning New Hampshire, Sanders packed the Mesquite Rodeo Arena, near Dallas, to rally voters before early voting began. His campaign also tapped into the grassroots support of progressive candidates for lower office by endorsing candidates in the Texas Democratic primaries.

The momentum behind Sanders in Nevada and Texas was also thought to be connected to the lack of support Biden received from Latino voters early in the primary. Our polls of registered voters prior to Super Tuesday in January and February captured the momentum for Sanders and shows the separation he was able to make after winning New Hampshire and starting his Texas campaign in mid-February. In late January, Sanders trailed Biden by 17 percent (35% to 18%) and Texas Latinos were split on whether they supported Biden (33%) or Sanders (30%). But when we checked in with all Texas voters one month later, support for Sanders had risen to 29 percent. Much of that increase is attributable to a 12 percent increase of Latino voters and 8 percent increase of Black voters saying they supported Sanders in February. As Biden fell to third place in Texas, he had temporarily lost support from Black voters who were considering a vote for Michael Bloomberg and Latino voters who were behind the new frontrunner. Had those numbers held and Texas voted before South Carolina, the entire nomination process for selecting the Democratic candidate could have been completely different.

The February polls by the *Dallas Morning News* and University of Texas at Tyler, and many other polls conducted after Iowa and New Hampshire, showed that the support Biden thought he had in Texas had slipped. The ability of South Carolina to bring Biden back showcased that he was a favored candidate among Black Democrats, which may have changed the dynamics of who voted on Super Tuesday. The real question of whether the outcome of the South Carolina Democratic primary on February 29 and the endorsement by O'Rourke on March 2 affected the outcome of the election on March 3 depends on how many ballots were cast during early voting and on Super Tuesday.

Voter enthusiasm was higher among Democratic primary voters because of the contested presidential primary. A comparison of ballots cast in both party primaries shows that 51 percent of the 4,111,595 primary voters voted on the Democratic side. Voter participation also illuminated other trends in early voting and absentee ballots most. Early voting in 2020 surpassed the total number of ballots cast in 2016, but 53 percent of all Republican primary ballots were cast early, and 52 percent of Democratic primary voters waited to vote in person on Election Day.

In the case of the 2020 Texas Democratic primary, voters waited to see if Biden could come back or were likely encouraged by the O'Rourke's endorsement the night before and the stories about Biden eating a late-night cheeseburger at Whataburger. The renewed enthusiasm of voters who realized the importance of their vote and determining who would receive delegates from the second largest state also dissuaded Republican voters from standing in long lines because the statewide Republican primaries were less competitive.

Super Tuesday's surge of voters in Texas does not mean that Bernie Sanders generated momentum within the progressive wing of Texas's electorate. Table 5.1 offers a comparison of how successful Biden and Sanders were in counties based on the enthusiasm of voters to cast their ballot early. Sanders received more votes than Biden in sixteen of the twenty-four counties that received at least 40 percent of the primary ballots before Election Day. Biden received more votes than Sanders in 90 percent of the counties where at least 60 percent of the voters were late deciders. As a result, Biden did better in Dallas, Harris, and Tarrant counties where O'Rourke's endorsement could have had a profound impact on turnout and vote choice.

Another key to Sander's potential was his popularity among Latino voters. On this question, the counties where Bernie Sanders did well point reinforce that this was the case. Sanders won large counties along the border like El Paso, Hidalgo, Webb, and most of the Borderland counties. He also won much of the I-35 corridor counties, including Bexar, Travis, and the growing counties of Hays and Williamson. The uniqueness of the Sanders coalition is that he was able to appeal to some large metropolitan areas and to the border counties where individual voters were more likely to use early voting in the Democratic primary more than other areas of the state. The realization that Sanders ran the strongest in areas where Latino residents live in concentrated areas hints that Latino enthusiasm for Sanders did not decline. One concern is that it will take more elections in the future for Latino voters across the state who identify as Democrats to provide the same level of turnout in primary elections as they do in general elections. The idea that there is not yet a critical mass to draw from is also consistent with our polling that shows Latino voters identify as pure Independents at a greater margin and fewer identify as Democrat than Black voters.

Table 5.1. Counties Where Sanders Led Biden or Biden Led Sanders, by Percentage of Votes Cast Early

Percentage of ballots cast early	Counties Sanders Led	Counties Biden Led
More than 50%	1	4
Between 40% and 49%	15	4
Between 30% and 39%	16	75
Between 20% and 29%	7	121
Between 0% and 19%	1	10
Total	40	214

Source: Analysis by the authors of county-level reports from the Texas Secretary of State's office.

The hard lesson of the 2020 presidential primary in Texas is that institutionally the election was a small step for Biden's comeback in the delegate count. Finishing first provided tremendous momentum nationally. The tally of all votes gave Biden 34 percent of all votes cast and Sanders 30 percent, yielding those candidates 113 delegates and ninety-nine delegates respectively. Mayor Mike Bloomberg was pledged eleven district-level delegates.[4] The split reflects the rules of the Texas Democratic presidential primary, which awards seventy-nine delegates proportionally to candidates who receive more than 15 percent of the statewide vote. The remaining 149 pledged delegates are proportionally distributed within geographic regions using the state party's formula to reward who wins one of the thirty-one Texas State Senate districts. Some state senate districts are worth more, based on how supportive the area was for the Democratic nominee in the two most recent statewide elections. The party also uses the 15 percent rule again to determine which candidates within a state senate district will receive a delegate. The cut-off was important, because Bloomberg fell 1 percent shy of receiving a share of the statewide delegates and was only able to receive support from some of the senate districts; moreover, candidates like Elizabeth Warren left Texas empty-handed.

What Were the Democratic Voters Looking for in a Nominee?

Once the televised debates of candidates for the Democratic nomination began in the summer of 2019, we began polling Texas voters about who they supported and what characteristics they felt were important for a nominee

Table 5.2. Preferred Candidate Characteristics among Democratic Voters in Texas

	Support Obama's policy legacy	Appeals to Independents	Closest to Me on Policy issues	Energize the Base
February 2020	39%	24%	23%	13%
January 2020	21	24	43	11

to have. Unsurprisingly in 2019, the leading answer among Democratic voters was that they wanted a nominee who was electable (45%) or a candidate to share their same policy views (33%). In 2020, Democratic voters in Texas indicated they were most interested in the policy positions of candidates, either to match with their own or to continue the work of President Obama.

In the weeks preceding the Super Tuesday election, voters began looking for different characteristics each month based on the context of the election. Each row in table 5.2 shows the changes we observed by asking the same question at two different points in the primary process. Prior to the Iowa Caucuses, Democratic voters in Texas held an individualistic view of what attributes a candidate should have. They wanted the nominee to have the same policy views they did. Once the delegate race had begun and voters knew who was in the lead after Iowa and New Hampshire, Texas Democratic voters focused their attention on which candidate would support the policy legacy of President Obama.

The shake up in the characteristics primary voters looked for in a nominee between January and February becomes interesting when we also look at which candidates those voters supported (table 5.3). By being a fierce proponent of expanding Medicare for all, Bernie Sanders became the favored candidate of 35 percent of voters who were seeking a candidate that would protect the legacy of President Obama's policies. Before he had won a primary, he was only supported by 13 percent of voters with the same opinion. In addition to encroaching on Biden's claim to the Obama legacy, more voters recognized they wanted a return to the previous administration at the same time Sanders was building momentum. As the election approached, Sanders was not the only candidate to draw support away from Biden in February. Biden's slide also meant that voters who identified as slightly liberal, moderate, and slightly

Table 5.3. Candidate Preference Based on the Most Important Characteristic to Voters

Question	Biden	Sanders	Warren	Bloomberg	All Others	Undecided	N
Policy (Jan)	28%	21%	16%	13%	11%	11%	213
Policy (Feb)	23	31	12	21	10	3	128
Appeal to Ind (Jan)	38	14	15	15	12	6	123
Appeal to Ind (Feb)	21	22	5	21	27	4	141
Obama's legacy (Jan)	32	13	10	18	17	10	85
Obama's legacy (Feb)	17	35	12	22	10	4	208

conservative slightly favored Mike Bloomberg in mid-February. Different constituencies were all reading the context of the election as Super Tuesday approached and began looking for other candidates they could support. After Sander's lead over Biden diminished, the election result was between what the two different polls showed, suggesting for many the temptation to support another candidate was short-lived.

Low Information Voting Down Ballot: The Power of Surnames

On the Democratic ballot with the presidential primary was a large field of candidates seeking the Democratic nomination to run against Senator John Cornyn (R). Twelve candidates entered the election, all needing to develop name recognition across the state. Overall, seven candidates measured more than 2 percent support within the electorate and no candidate received more than 15 percent support in the polls. Most voters responded to the poll that they simply did not know enough about the twelve candidates to decide, including 56 percent in January and 46 percent during early voting. This made the election ripe for a few common patterns to emerge. First, it was clear there would be a run-off election. Second, without significant name recognition to differentiate the candidates and no difference in the party labels, voters looked for other cues to determine their support. The two most powerful cues were race and surname.[5]

The candidates who survey respondents supported in the poll had a wide range of backgrounds. The ballot included former U.S. Representative Chris Bell (2003–2005), Houston City Council member Amanda Edwards, veteran helicopter pilot MJ Hegar, State Senator Royce West, activist Christina Tzintzún Ramirez, Sema Hernandez, and Annie "Mamá" Garcia among others. The impact of any national endorsements was muddled when the Texas Democratic Senate primary became a proxy battle for the future of the national party. Initially, Minority Leader Chuck Schumer (D-NY) and the Democratic Senatorial Campaign Committee boosted MJ Hegar's electability with an endorsement. Closer to the election, Representative Alexandra Ocasio-Cortez (D-NY) endorsed Christina Tzintzún Ramirez to promote the importance of mobilizing young voters and Latinos in Texas to elect a more progressive candidate.

The Democratic electorate became divided along racial and ethnic lines on who they would support in the Senate primary. White Democratic voters were largely behind MJ Hegar (24%), and 44 percent were still unsure. Black Democratic voters supported Senator Royce West (15%) most often and were a core constituency of Amanda Edwards (7%). Latino voters showed the strongest support for Tzintzún Ramirez (13%) and the largest levels of support for political newcomers Annie "Mamá" Garcia (7%) and former Senate candidate Sema Hernandez (5%).

Candidate support in the Senate primary also frequently matched the region that a candidate had served. Senator West received strong support from the Dallas region, which he represents in the state senate. He received endorsements from high-profile Black residents of the city like Emmitt Smith and the *Dallas Morning News* Editorial Board who endorsed West and Amanda Edwards in the primary.[6] Christina Tzintzún Ramirez focused on mobilizing Latino voters in large cities in South Texas and El Paso where she already had momentum from her career protecting the rights of undocumented workers and registering voters with Jolt. Finally, Central Texas Democrats continued to support Hegar in the primary after Democrats in the 31st District nominated her to run against Representative John Carter (R) in 2018.

As expected, Hegar moved onto the primary run-off with 22 percent of the vote. The race with Hegar's opponent was close between West (15%) and Tzintzún Ramirez (13%). West advanced, which raises the question, did the fourth-place candidate Annie "Mamá" Garcia (10%) cost Tzintzún

Ramirez votes? The two candidates had a tense relationship. In an interview with the *Austin American-Statesman*, Garcia said that she added "Mamá" to her name on the ballot because "she was inspired by Brad 'Scarface' Jordan, a rapper who ran for Houston City Council last year. (He lost in the run-off.)"[7] The two female candidates were connected throughout the campaign, since Ramirez apologized for a joke she would offer at campaign gatherings: "Tzintzún is more Mexican than any Garcia or Lopez. We were the only indigenous group in Mexico that were not defeated by the Aztecs. So, you know I come from good lineage and I'm ready to defeat John Cornyn."[8] The ballots cast in a crowded and low-information election, and the controversy between two candidates, shows that surnames do attract support and candidates recognize the power of that recognition.

The public frequently is less informed about the incumbents and their challengers for lower offices. Throughout 2020, O'Rourke continued his efforts to mobilize voters by directly reaching out to them with the Powered by the People organization to support candidates for the Texas House. The ambitious goal of the Texas Democratic Party was to recruit candidates and try to win enough seats to win a majority of the Texas State House. During the year, voters in the state were equally divided about which party they wanted to win control of the chamber. These elections are won district by district so we asked a more direct question to see if voters would be more likely to support a candidate for the State House if someone else with high name recognition endorsed them. In February, 43 percent of independent voters said they would support a candidate for the State House if O'Rourke visited their district. Visits by O'Rourke were also a key mechanism to bolster enthusiasm for a candidate within the Democratic primary because 89 percent of Democratic voters said they would be likely to support a candidate supported by Powered by the People.

Incumbency in the 2020 Republican Nomination for the U.S. Senate

As twelve candidates campaigned to challenge Senator John Cornyn (R-TX), the incumbent senator easily retained his nomination in the primary election. The campaign still had drama because of party activists. At the 2018 Texas Republican Convention, Senator Cornyn was booed by some of the attendees there to celebrate Senator Cruz's nomination. This dissent within the party faithful fueled speculation that the three-term senator may face a strong primary challenge.

Four candidates, emerged to challenge Cornyn, who had won the 2014 Republican nomination with 59 percent of the vote.. The challengers, Dwayne Stovall, Mark Yancey, John Anthony Castro, and Virgil Bierschwale all lacked the equivalent political experience and name recognition the incumbent had. This was Stovall's second time challenging Cornyn in a Senate primary after receiving 11 percent of the vote in 2014. In 2020, Stovall echoed the rhetoric of President Trump that the Left sought to destroy liberty and earned the endorsement of a Tea Party organization in East Texas, Grassroots America: We the People. Other candidates also adopted aspects of populist rhetoric including Mark Yancey, who campaigned on the need for term limits to highlight the length of Cornyn's eighteen-year career in the Senate. John Anthony Castro boasted a message of trying to eliminate corruption in Washington, D.C.

Almost assured of his renomination, Senator Cornyn's campaign remained relatively quiet. This meant that none of the statewide elections in the Republican primary, for president or Senate, were working to activate turnout on a large scale. In fact, public comments by Senator Cornyn were most often directed at the candidates on the Democratic side. By ignoring the other candidates, the most common information voters had on which to base their candidate preference was whether they trusted another candidate to be a better representative of Texas than Senator Cornyn had been. Respondents to the *Dallas Morning News*/UT Tyler polls in January and February both showed that 56 percent of the registered voters who might vote in the 2020 Senate Republican Primary supported Senator Cornyn and at least 35 percent were not sure who they would vote for. In the January poll, John Anthony Castro received the second most support but was 52 percent behind Cornyn. That same distance in the polls existed in February when voters who opposed Cornyn were slightly more likely to support Dwayne Stovall over John Anthony Castro (table 5.4).

The clearest difference between Texas's Senate Republican primary in 2020 and the Lieutenant Governor Republican primary in 2014 is the number of challengers with prior elected experience who emerged to seek the nomination. Lieutenant Governor Dewhurst was forced into a run-off election because he faced three challengers who had won elections to serve in the state government. Senator John Cornyn was in a much better position because

Table 5.4. Preference of Texas Republican Voters for the Republican Nomination for U.S. Senate, 2020

	Cornyn	Stovall	Yancey	Castro	Bierschwale	Not Sure
February 2020	56%	4%	2%	3%	0%	35%
January 2020	56	2	1	4	1	36

ambitious candidates strategically chose not to challenge the well-known candidate who has been among the most popular elected officials in Texas for much of the decade because of his appeal to Independents and Republicans.

The survey preferences of Republican primary voters about the candidates for the Republican nomination for president replicated the responses observed in the Senate race (table 5.5). The clear contrast was President Donald Trump's style to Senator Cornyn's calm demeanor. Later in the campaign, Senator Cornyn expressed his relationship with President Trump had been frustrating at times. During an interview with the *Fort Worth Star-Telegram* Cornyn said he was initially optimistic; "Maybe like a lot of women who get married and think they're going to change their spouse, and that doesn't usually work out very well."[9]

The benefit for Trump is that he built a coalition of voters who supported him or strategically voted in favor of him because there was no viable alternative in the 2020 primary.[10] As a first-time candidate, Trump struggled in the 2016 Texas Republican primary, receiving 27 percent and coming in second to Senator Ted Cruz (44 percent). In the 2020 Texas Republican primary, President Trump was the head of the Republican Party and had the ability to dissuade strong candidates from entering the primary.

The consistent value of a party label to attract voters has encouraged many ambitious candidates to act strategically. For Republicans, being a strategic

Table 5.5. Preference of Texas Republican Voters for President, Republican Nomination in 2020

	Trump	Weld	Walsh	Sanford	Not Sure
February 2020	86%	6%	—	—	8%
January 2020	82	2	4	—	11
November 2019	78	1	1	4	16

candidate means waiting to file for an election once the incumbent has re-
tired or left the office to run for another position. Ambitious candidates
who are not Republicans will likely seek the Democratic nomination, so that
they can survive the primary and live to compete in the general election. The
conditional nature of how candidates assess the best path to being competitive in the election has led to elections where Republicans are most clearly
tested in their first primary election and then rarely receive a strong challenge
thereafter.

What Are Voters Going to Look for Next in a Nominee?

After the 2020 election, we surveyed registered voters in Texas once more, in
April 2021. This time we asked voters if the 2022 primary were held today,
would you vote in the Democratic primary, Republican primary, or not vote
in the election? From this question we got a glimpse of how Texans would
vote in a post-Trump election with respect to which primary they would
choose and what characteristics they would prefer a nominee to have.

Far ahead of knowing who would be on the ballot, most Texas voters continued to expect they would choose to vote in the Republican primary (45%)
over the Democratic primary (40%), as shown in table 5.6. The overall breakdown suggests that Democratic candidates still face the difficult task of attracting more Independent voters to help select their nominees. Also, the difficulty in mobilizing Latino voters to participate in the Democratic primary
rests in the ambivalence Latino voters have in choosing the nominee. Moreover, the time invested in mobilizing Latino voters may not actually yield
more ballots for the Democratic candidate as only 5 percent more Latinos
said they would plan to vote in the Democratic primary. The party also faces
similar problems with Asian American voters who said they would opt out
of voting in a primary 10 percent more often than all voters. Unsurprisingly,
most White voters will still opt to participate in the Republican primary. The
problem for moderate Republican candidates is that more Republicans than
Democrats indicated that they would skip the primary.

In addition to the meaningful differences in how future primary election
constituencies may look in the future, Texas Democrats and Texas Republicans have clear preferences on what they would like to see in a future nominee
for governor. A majority of voters who would participate in the Democratic
primary (51%) said that they would prefer a progressive candidate to win the

Table 5.6. Primary Election Choice of Texas Voters, 2021

Primary	Total	Latino	Black	Asian	White	Dem	Indep.	Rep.
Democratic	40%	43%	72%	41%	32%	93	29%	5%
Republican	45	38	16	34	55	3	34	89
Would not vote	15	21	12	25	13	4	37	6

Democratic nomination. The rest of the Democratic constituency was split between not knowing what they wanted and wanting a centrist (25%). Latino voters (56%) also indicated they wanted a progressive candidate, as did voters who self-described themselves as liberals (66%). The Independent candidate preferences that are forming among Latinos and liberals within the Democratic primary electorate are distinctly different from the past coordination of Democratic elites to coalesce support around a centrist candidate. The empowerment of a new Democratic base may itself be a legacy of the unsuccessful campaigns by Bernie Sanders and Christina Tzintzún Ramirez in Texas.

We asked Republican voters a separate follow up question, which acknowledged the common case that an incumbent would be seeking the nomination. In this case, Governor Greg Abbott was the most recognizable nominee. A plurality of Republican primary voters wanted to nominate Governor Abbott again (47%). Within some of the most influential constituencies of the Texas Republican primary, Abbott received support from most voters including 54 percent of all conservative voters, 58 percent of evangelicals, and 58 percent of voters older than sixty-five. Opposition to the governor was diffuse, with 20 percent of the primary electorate preferring a centrist, 14 percent hoping for someone more conservative than Abbott, and 18 percent who wanted the next nominee to be more like Donald Trump.

Discussion and Conclusion

Presently the traditional base of both political parties in Texas is large enough to dictate the outcome of a primary election when there are not three or more strong candidates in a contest. This supports the notion that the median voter in the primary election matters a great deal, even if the median is more extreme than the incumbent candidate.

Up to now, the two major parties in Texas have preserved broader ideological diversity within their ranks than most states. Texas's Democratic Party has a growing and emboldened progressive wing, which is growing because of the engagement of voters outside of the major metropolitan areas. Voters in the Texas Democratic Party still frequently fall in line with candidates that prioritize the bipartisanship and pragmatism like MJ Hegar and Beto O'Rourke. As a long-standing minority party these candidates can hold broader appeal within the Democratic electorate because there is an interest by the party to win elections by running candidates who might appeal to Independent voters. As Texas Republicans have held power in the state for longer periods of time, the power of the party label itself appears to allow primary voters to vote more sincerely for which candidate matches their personal policy views. This typically gives an advantage to conservative candidates, but the diversity within the Republican Party guards against nominating a more extreme candidate when turnout is normal.

The Trump presidency added a new stream of populism in two different primary election cycles for the Texas Republican Party. But when primary voters were offered a more traditional candidate to choose from, like John Cornyn, that candidate won the primary by a wide margin. This is why traditional partisans often remained safe from losing to a candidate who appeals to a coalition of the extremes in both parties.[11] The electorate of extremely conservative voters are not overtly dissatisfied with the attention they get from conservative Republicans in Texas and 2021 polling suggests that only 18 percent of Republicans are looking for a candidate to govern Texas like President Trump did at the national level. Both Cornyn and Abbott used aspects of their incumbency to distance themselves from President Trump and still succeed electorally.

In this chapter we assessed how important the conditions of a primary election are to whomever receives the party nomination. We showed that candidates who are strongly supported by the party establishment can be most vulnerable in a party primary if voters believe that the candidate is out of step with the average primary voter and multiple strong candidates emerge. Because state level elections are typically environments where voters have little to no information about all the candidates, both points are important. If insurgent Republican candidates can continue to force run-off elections in the primaries, there is a chance that polarization will continue to increase within the state.

The key concern for Republicans and Democrats within the state is whether Independent voters or Republican voters who are not strong in their partisanship will continue to support candidates who begin to move the state further to the right. A look back to the general election results of 2018, where Trump ally and Attorney General Ken Paxton (R) won reelection with 50.5 percent of the vote and Land Commissioner George P. Bush (R) won reelection with 54 percent of the vote, suggests that in a low-information environment the bluster of a candidate can tarnish the advantage of the party label.

CHAPTER 6

A Sleeping Giant

The Changing Electorate

Poking the big red elephant might get you trampled.
—Gromer Jeffers, Jr. 2020[1]

P
URPLE STATES ARE WHERE Democrats and Republicans have an almost equal say in their elections. Candidates from both parties are typically able to win elections and incumbents become less safe. The electorate in Texas is shifting, but in ways that make it more difficult for political parties to predict the outcome of an election for their candidates. Texas Democrats have not won a statewide election to establish a leader who speaks on behalf of the party.

The trend of electoral success for Republicans has persisted despite a substantial number of Texans identifying as pure Independents and finding fault in the direction that Republicans are leading the state as laws move to become more conservative. Republicans are holding onto their statewide offices because party candidates have significant advantages from incumbency or prior experience by serving in another role. Even as the electoral margins get closer in Texas, Governor Abbott's chief consultant claimed the 2020 elections were a realization that, "We had great candidates and a good message and they worked hard as a team."[2] The work to turn a state purple requires that voters recognize a candidate's strengths and in this state someone has a record to deflect the claim of being too liberal.

The Texas Democratic Party has worked hard to mobilize voters in the six most populous counties through the project Battleground Texas but are still working to develop the resources to learn about the rest of the state. As a result of those efforts, the editor of *Inside Election*, Nathan Gonzalez, said, "We simply have to get beyond the picture in our head of Texas being a giant red state, when in reality it is a big red state with growing islands of blue in the metropolitan areas."[3] Each election offers a new opportunity to assess expectations, but Democratic strategist Matt Angle described 2020 as "the biggest gap between expectations and results."[4]

The path to recognizing Texas as a battleground state requires that a split in the vote share be less than 5 percent between the first place and second place candidate for president. In 2020, the gap between President Donald Trump and former Vice President Joe Biden was 5.5 percent in an election that saw greater voter turnout than previous presidential elections. The expectation that Texas is even more politically competitive is a result of the 2018 election, which saw a difference of 2.6 percent between Senator Ted Cruz and challenger Representative Beto O'Rourke. The midyear election result was the closest race in Texas for the U.S. Senate since 1978. The increasing competition in Texas's election led the *Cook Political Report* to identify Texas as a toss-up state in the 2020 presidential election because of the 2018 election and preelection polls that showed Biden was catching up to Trump.

After the election, Nathan Gonzalez was quick to remind the public, "It's going to take a couple more election cycles to know how much this movement was personal to Trump and how much of it was a broader trend towards the Democratic Party."[5] It is wise to see this time of turbulent change in the electorate with patience, but Gonzalez's point alludes to the interest that political analysts have in understanding who is making Texas politically competitive and have recent events been large enough to shift viewpoints in the long term. Because of course, these shifts could reflect candidate-centered politics where voters may have liked O'Rourke more than other Democratic candidates.

Recognizing How the Electorate Is Different from the Population

It is common to mention how Texas is more diverse than the nation. The 2010 Census found that there was no majority group in the population based on race and ethnicity. Ten years later, the 2020 Census indicated that the non-Hispanic white population was only half a percent larger than the Hispanic

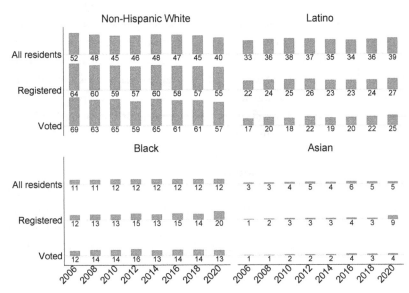

Source: Census and Current Population Survey

Figure 6.1. Proportion of Race and Ethnic Groups in Texas's Population,
by Political Participation

population. The impact of this diversity on the electorate has lagged for two reasons. First, the growth of the Latino community includes individuals under the age of eighteen. Second, it takes time for new Texans and younger voters to become civically engaged by registering to vote and participating in elections. When combined, these two explanations can exacerbate the underrepresentation of a community in politics.

We see an imbalance of political participation by race and ethnicity emerge in figure 6.1. The non-Hispanic white population was afforded a 17 percent increase in the weight of its political voice from 2006 to 2020 based on the difference between who voted and who lived in the state. Whites registered to vote at higher rates and vote at higher rates in Texas. Black voters also exhibit a more powerful force in the elections than the total population may imply. A notable difference between the White and Black populations of the state is that Blacks consistently make up the same proportion of the electorate, but White voters make up less of the Texas electorate each election.

The most striking difference across the race and ethnic groups is the lagging political participation of Latinos in Texas. Typically, pundits focus on the realization that Latinos do not make up more than 30 percent of the electorate and pin the future of Texas politics on when this electorate will awaken. The trends we can see over time in figure 6.1 show this is an outdated argument. The Latino voting bloc is already awakening. Campaign strategists now simply need to think about what the ceiling of the increasing Latino turnout will be. Texas Latinos already make up 8 percent more of all ballots cast in the elections after President George W. Bush was reelected.

The declining share of ballots cast by White voters, in exchange for more ballots being cast by Latino voters, sets a new landscape as Texas becomes more politically competitive. We will shed light on how these new voters are shifting the political foundations and have helped elect leaders in the past. Are ideology and religion offering new bridges for candidates to appeal to a changing electorate?

Difference of Choices: Governor and Senator

The 2018 election had two high profile elections to attract the interest of voters. Senator Ted Cruz was challenged by U.S. Representative Beto O'Rourke, who was the first Democratic nominee to run for a Senate seat from Texas with experience in Washington, D.C. since Senator Lloyd Bentsen was reelected in 1988. Governor Greg Abbott was challenged by former Dallas County sheriff Lupe Valdez, who had spoken at the Democratic National Convention in 2016 and was the first Latino to run for governor since Tony Sanchez failed to connect with the Latino electorate in 2002.[6] Valdez is also one of only two Latina candidates to win the nomination for a major party in Texas, along with State Supreme Court Justice Eva Guzman. The campaign began with low expectations that the Democratic nominees could compete but ended with a much closer race than anticipated. The momentum was largely based on the popularity of O'Rourke relative to Cruz. It was generated by O'Rourke's high-energy and willingness to speak to often-ignored communities, even if his speeches often used variations of one four-letter word as a primary adjective to describe an issue.

The 2018 Senate and governor races were much more similar than anticipated. Still, the marginal benefits a candidate can receive by increasing their name recognition were apparent. Zach Malitz, a campaign advisor to O'Rourke reflected on the race to say, "If you spend seriously here, Texas is a competitive state."[7] In the governors' race, Greg Abbott won 55.8 percent of all votes, while Democrat Lupe Valdez won 42.5 percent of all ballots cast. In the senate race, 50.9 percent of voters supported Senator Cruz and O'Rourke won 48.3 percent of all votes cast. Both winners benefitted from the conservative nature of the state, but some Independents and Republicans split their ticket between Governor Abbott and O'Rourke.

Our own UT Tyler poll from October 2018 found significant predictors of a voter's preference of candidates that went beyond party. Black and Latino voters were both less likely to support Abbott and Cruz, which supports the idea that changing demographics and a triethnic electorate are contributing to closer election outcomes. Abbott and Cruz held back the tide of a competitive election with the support of voters who found religion to be an important part of their life. Male voters were also an important block of voters for Republicans. Male voters supported Cruz over O'Rourke 15 percent more often than female voters in Texas (63% of males to 48% of females). The 13 percent gender gap in the governor's race also strongly favored Abbott, who received support from 70 percent of male voters and 57 percent of female voters.

Figuring out what makes voters prefer a particular candidate requires more detail than partisanship in a state like Texas where some Republicans seem to fare well and others are becoming more vulnerable. The simplest way to think about this is to simultaneously compare the importance of a voter's race, party identification, ideology, the importance of religion in one's life, and gender. When we do this, shifts in the electorate can be defined with more detail. Accounting for the personal characteristics of a voter increases the ability to predict who a voter will choose for governor by 53 percent when the choice is between Sheriff Lupe Valdez and Governor Abbott. Abbott's bipartisan appeal means that a random choice would have only correctly predicted 36 percent of Texas voters, but the model is able to explain the behavior of 89.1 percent of voters. In a contest where the challenger is not defined as being "too liberal" and the incumbent is more polarizing to Independents, that same model improves our ability to predict a voter's preference by 29 percent, 90 percent from the model and 61 percent from a random selection.

Updating Our Understanding of 2018 with 2020

The dynamics were exceptionally different for the 2020 elections. It would have been different simply because of the changes a campaign could have planned for: a new law ended straight ticket voting in Texas after 2019 and 2020 would have higher turnout for a presidential year. The exceptional difference of the 2020 election was the backdrop of a hotly contested race for president and a public affected by the COVID-19 pandemic.

The presidential election placed President Trump on the ballot, which engaged voters of both parties and Independents as well. Approval for President Trump was consistently 10 percent harsher than how the public evaluated Governor Abbott during the year of 2020. As president, Trump did not centralize power to respond to the public health emergency; he chose to delegate it to the states. Governor Abbott, in turn, declared a state of emergency and allowed counties to determine details of curfews and stay-at-home orders in March until establishing a stay-at-home order for the state of Texas for the month of April. Texans experienced the major economic disruptions from supply chain issues and hoarding of staples like toilet paper and limits on capacity for public places. Those issues contributed to a record high of 12.9 percent in the unemployment rate in April 2020, an increase of 9 percent from the unemployment rate of 3.7 percent two months before.[8] In November 2020, the unemployment rate was 5.7 percent lower than the start of the initial shock of the pandemic creating a volatile environment where the economy showed signs of improving differently in sectors and regions of the state throughout the year. For retrospective voters who evaluate the strength of the economy, Texas was certainly in dire need of recovery to return to a time when the unemployment rate was at a record low of 3.7 percent in November 2018.

Republican and Democratic campaigns set two different visions to run their campaigns. Texas Republicans drafted behind President Trump by returning to the campaign trail in person in June of 2020. The president returned to the campaign trail on June 11 for a fundraiser in Dallas at a private home. Following guidelines from the Centers for Disease Control and Prevention, attendance at the fundraiser was limited to twenty-five individuals and the expected contribution from attendees was raised to $580,600 per couple.[9] President Trump returned to again in early July to speak at the Conservative Political Action Conference, hosted in Dallas. Other fundraisers in

Texas were quickly added to the schedule with visits to Odessa in late July. The visits were not without criticism, as Texas accounted for 16 percent of all COVID-19 infections reported across the country after the July 4 holiday.[10] President Trump's strategy to go to the public to keep the economy open in places like Texas, Arizona, Florida, and Georgia made his campaign a return to a normal campaign while Texas Democrats were cautious and reached out to voters remotely.

Planning the next step for a campaign must have seemed uncertain as business owners faced choices about the potential consequences of closing or enforcing mask mandates. Another shock was that July 2020 blended two contexts: a spike in COVID-19 peaked and a start to the general election. The *Dallas Morning News*/UT Tyler poll found that challenger Joe Biden (46%) held a 5 percent lead over President Donald Trump among registered voters in Texas. Future polls did not capture this lead again, but the public's choice between the two candidates began to narrow as the number of COVID-19 infections declined. A primary driver of this was a split in the frame of how voters understood the pandemic. In July 2020, more than 85 percent of voters strongly agreed (64%) or agreed (21%) that the COVID-19 pandemic was a major threat. These voters were the most critical of Donald Trump, with a majority indicating they would vote for Joe Biden (50%) over the president (36%). Two months later in September, Biden's lead was only 1 percent, and 80 percent of voters strongly agreed (58 percent) or agreed (22%) that the pandemic was still a major threat. Trump's summer and fall slump continued because Texas voters who saw the pandemic as a major threat continued to support Biden by a wide margin (52% for Biden, 37% for Trump).

A clear theme of Texas Democrats was to keep the public's focus on the public health crisis to settle the uncertainty that was creating economic instability. President Trump deflected the long-term threat of the pandemic to bolster beliefs that places like Texas could return to their record growth in short order, if he were reelected. This gave Republican incumbent Senator John Cornyn and Governor Abbott a path to show empathy to Texans during a health crisis and encourage the hospitality industry to replace the 577,200 jobs that were lost between March and April of 2020 in Texas.[11] Maintaining a focus on the stewardship of the economy offered a contrasting dimension to discuss current events that Texas Republicans had more familiarity with. Despite the harsh evaluations of the leadership of how elected leaders responded to the COVID-19 pandemic, 52 percent of voters said they trusted President

Donald Trump to handle the economy more than Joe Biden (47%). Interestingly, this 5 percent difference between the two candidates on the economy revealed the most accurate prediction of the preelection polls.

Experiences from the pandemic hardened the political views of many, and Texans witnessed a political dialogue where candidates ultimately spoke past one another by emphasizing separate policy dimensions that presented their best opportunity for success. Campaigns were in the business of shifting how voters saw current events (health and financial security), rather than persuading voters that the candidate had a better plan for what the voter cared about. This raised questions about whether Senator Cornyn would become vulnerable with Donald Trump on the ticket. The converse later appeared to be true. Early in the campaign Donald Trump Jr. declared Senator Cornyn was one of his father's biggest allies.[12] Cornyn led his own get-out-the-vote effort to gain support from 53.5 percent of the voters, which was a benefit to President Trump who received 52 percent of the votes in his contest.

Education, marital status, and religious beliefs were more influential in shaping the 2020 electorate differently than the 2018 election. Education was negatively correlated with support for Trump. Increasing levels of education were slightly more highly correlated with favoring Biden. For most of the period since World War II, more highly educated voters have backed GOP candidates, and less educated voters have tended to favor Democrats.[13] Married respondents were more likely to support Trump, and unmarried respondents were more likely to support Biden. A striking difference with the 2020 electorate from the traditional cultural influence was the break of mainline Protestants from the Republican nominee. Joe Biden received slightly more support from mainline Protestants (Methodists, Episcopalians, and the like) than respondents of other religious affiliations. These factors were influential, but all three were less predictive than knowing a person's partisanship and ideology.[14]

At first look, it may seem like President Trump and Senator Cornyn's fate were tied together. Trump lost twenty-two of Texas's 254 counties and Cornyn lost twenty-one counties, three more than he lost in 2014. Cornyn's ability to run ahead of the presidential candidate was through appeals to voters on the margins. Voters did not show significant differences based on marriage or religious affiliations, but they did by gender. Men were slightly more likely to favor the incumbent Senator John Cornyn than women, suggesting

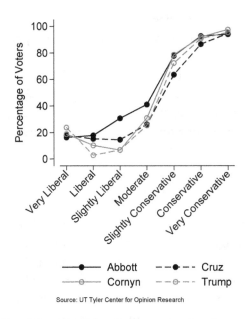

Figure 6.2. Republican Candidate Preference, 2018 and 2020, by Ideology

that a female candidate like military veteran MJ Hegar found a new dimension to compete with Senator Cornyn where prior candidates had not.

Ideology continued to play a huge role in candidate preference, even after controlling for partisanship.[15] Figure 6.2 reveals that Republican candidates do not do well with liberals, and most—excluding Greg Abbott<em dash>do not do all that well with moderates, either. The relationships here are not perfectly linear, particularly since the three categories of liberal respondents show support for Republicans at levels that don't always make sense, but are, in the end, uniformly low. Then the move from liberal to moderate and on up to very conservative respondents is more highly correlated with support for Republican candidates, in a linear fashion.

Governor Abbott is the most uniformly popular of the four Republican incumbents. Support for Abbott is less dependent on the ideology of the respondents and relatively high in most categories, especially for liberals and moderates. Support for, and opposition to Trump was the most polarized in terms of ideology. The finding that 23.8 percent of very liberal voters supported Trump over Biden is more likely to be related to measurement error because there are fewer "very liberal" voters in Texas. President Trump, with no ties to Texas, received nominal support from those responding as "liberal" or "slightly liberal."

Senator Cornyn, who has proven to be unbeatable in normal circumstances, was exceptionally popular among conservatives, but unable to achieve similar levels of support among liberal voters that Senator Cruz received in 2018. This could be a referendum for having President Trump on the ticket and the full realization of Democratic support in the most populated counties.

The Big Change

A remarkable realization is that the views of partisans and ideologues are not changing during this shift in Texas's political culture, rather the size each partisan or ideological group is changing. This resembles a situation where parties are defining themselves in relation to one another and voters are learning where they fit in Texas's new political landscape. One way to see the diversity of political preferences that exist is to consider how religious beliefs vary in intensity and denomination.

Voters who are the most devout and active in their faith support Republican candidates most often, but only Governor Abbott was able to appeal to voters who revealed their religion and said "religion provides some guidance" in their lives. After discussing the impact of religiosity on the future of Texas politics, we will explore differences in the political beliefs of evangelical Protestants, Roman Catholics, mainline Protestants, and those with no religious affiliation. A glance at figure 6.3 shows that increasing religiosity generally results in more pro-Republican voter preference, but this is especially the case in 2018. Religiosity is somewhat important in explaining candidate preference, but it pales in importance when compared with party identification and ideology.

The figures for individual candidates, Governor Abbott is the most favored candidate in general, and for all categories of voters except the least religious (who are most favorable to Cornyn). In all cases save one (Abbott in 2018), those who said religion was not important or provided only some guidance favored Democratic candidates. Those respondents who said religion provided quite a bit of guidance or a great deal of guidance, preferred the Republicans. We also found that Senator Cruz had less support than other Republicans from those who thought religion was not important in the 2018

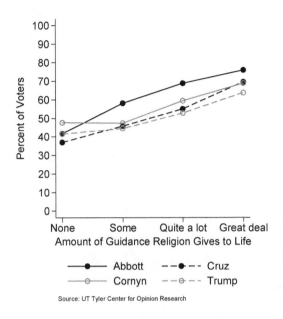

Figure 6.3. Republican Candidate Preference, 2018 and 2020, by Religiosity

race against O'Rourke, while both Abbott and Cruz had strong support from the very religious in 2018. We might ascertain from figure 6.3 that religiosity was more important in 2018 than in 2020, as party cues, ideology, and support or opposition to President Trump were the far more important variables in the highly polarized election of 2020.

The views of the electorate are also shifting within groups of voters, as categorized by their religious affiliation. Figure 6.3 illustrates how the political views of religious voters are not always consistently aligned across party identification, approval of the Republican governor, and approval of the president. The trend lines reflect views of voters by religion regarding affiliation with the Republican Party (black line) and approval of the President (dashes) from October 2018 to September 2019. Voter support for Governor Abbott (gray line) is available between September 2019 and September 2021, to reflect the start of when this question was added to the surveys.

The surveys in 2021 show the greatest change in this contrast because of the transition from President Trump to President Biden. In this transition,

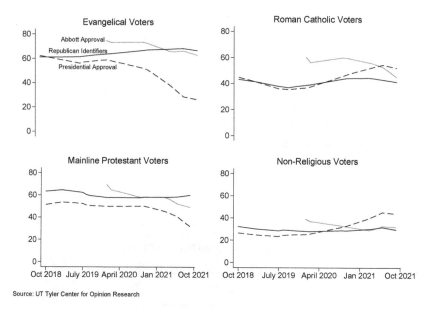

Source: UT Tyler Center for Opinion Research

Figure 6.4. Differences in Political Views, by Religious Denomination

Roman Catholic voters and nonreligious voters elevated their evaluation of the president, whereas Protestants (evangelicals and mainline) did not (figure 6.4). The time comparison also uncovers something else that is interesting. The partisan attitudes of religious voters and nonreligious voters remained stable throughout this period, even as the issues up for debate in Texas changed. One consequence of a shifting agenda is that we see approval of Governor Abbott declined after the 2020 election. This reflects the activity of the 87th Legislature when lawmakers claimed they had produced the most conservative legislative session in Texas's history. The timing also reflects a difference of opinions when Governor Abbott worked as an ally with a Republican president and when his power was challenged by a Democratic president.

The last comparison we investigate is gender. We have seen a gender gap that is sometimes small, sometimes large, where men are more prone to support Republicans and women are more likely to vote for Democrats over the last few decades. The gender gap began to emerge in the 1970s and has been consistently present in presidential elections, but it remains smaller (in the aggregate, at least) in congressional elections (figure 6.5).[16]

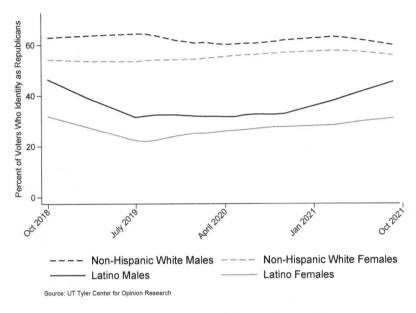

Figure 6.5 Gender Gap, among White and Latino Voters

Public concern for the COVID-19 replaced border security as a policy topic at the top of the minds of most voters. That said, the public's attitude toward whether a border wall along the Texas-Mexico border remained remarkably consistent between February 2019 and September 2021. The issue lingers as an unfinished project where those who believe a wall is necessary for a secure border reward a candidate who advocates for that position. An aggregation of survey responses from six surveys (2019–2021), suggests that 71 percent of those who at least agree that a wall along the Texas-Mexico border is necessary approve of Governor Abbott. In those same surveys, 54 percent of voters who believe a wall is not necessary disapprove of the governor. That comparison is truly a contrast of the actions the governor took in the 87th legislative session.

Once Texas began to use state funds and Governor Abbott began raising private funds for the project in 2021, there was a 6 percent increase in the number of voters who were neutral about the border wall. In 2021, the belief among registered voters that a wall was not necessary for a secure border fell 4 percent (from 38 percent in 2020) and support for the wall fell 2 percent (from 49% in 2020). The greatest change was not how actions by the state government affected perspectives on the border wall, it was how views on the border wall began to reflect approval for the governor. When President Trump was the focal point of extending the border barrier in Texas, only 40 percent of those who did not believe a wall was necessary disapproved of the governor. Once Abbott became the primary foil to President Biden's approach to border security, more than 64 percent of those who opposed a border wall also disapproved of Governor Abbott. The 24 percent decline in approval on one side of the coin was balanced by a 2 percent increase in approval from the declining population of voters who believed a wall was necessary.

A wall on Texas's border is only one of the questions leaders must contend with. The deferred action for childhood arrivals (DACA) is an immigration application process that applies to Texas residents who arrived in the United States illegally as children and grew up in the United States. The Dreamers program is less divisive among registered voters than the border wall and an issue Senator John Cornyn has worked on to support legislation.[17] The partisan divide of those who support a path to citizenship for Dreamers is 17 percent smaller (61% Democratic, 26% Republican) than the partisan divide among those who believe a border wall is necessary (19% Democratic, 71% Republican). Advocating for two independent ideas, forgiving immigration laws and secure borders, is a tight rope walk Republicans must maintain in order to appeal to pure Independents who marginally support DACA, believe a wall on the border is a good idea, or are ambivalent to the policy issue entirely. A concern with nationalizing either is that responses to control immigration appear less welcoming, be they trips by President Trump to McAllen or creating new processing centers as refugees seek asylum by coming to the Texas border.

General Elections Before, During, and After Trump in Texas

The realization that Texas has become a toss-up and battleground state is less surprising if we reflect on outcomes from nine recent statewide elections. Looking at the two-party vote, the share of votes a candidate got among those cast for a Republican or Democrat, we can see that Texas's trend toward becoming a purple state accelerated after the 2018 election (table 6.1). All three of Texas's recent incumbents—Governor Greg Abbott, Senator John Cornyn, and Senator Ted Cruz—won their elections prior to this period with large majorities. Ted Cruz won 58.2 percent of the two-party vote against Paul

Table 6.1. Presidential, U.S. Senate, and Gubernatorial Elections in Texas, 2012–2020, Two-Party Vote Percentages

Election	Democrat	Dem. Vote	Republican	Rep. Vote
2012 President	Barack Obama	42.0%	Mitt Romney	58.0%
2012 Senate	Paul Sadler	41.8	Ted Cruz	58.2
2014 Senate	David Alameel	35.8	John Cornyn	64.2
2014 Governor	Wendy Davis	39.6	Greg Abbott	60.4
2016 President	Hillary Clinton	45.3	Donald Trump	54.7
2018 Senate	Beto O'Rourke	48.7	Ted Cruz	51.3
2018 Governor	Lupe Valdez	43.2	Greg Abbott	56.8
2020 President	Joe Biden	47.2	Donald Trump	52.8
2020 Senate	MJ Hegar	45.1	John Cornyn	54.9

Sadler in 2012, and in 2014 John Cornyn won 64.2 percent of the two-party vote against David Alameel, while Greg Abbott won 60.4 percent of the two-party vote in his race with Wendy Davis. After Trump won Texas (and the presidency) in 2016, Abbott, Cruz, and Cornyn all won reelection again, but each won with lower two-party vote percentages after the 2016 Trump victory. The 2020 election also showed that Donald Trump underperformed in Texas by defeating Joe Biden by 3.8 percent less of the two-party vote than Trump received in 2016.

The relative strength or weakness of a candidate who challenges an incumbent makes all the difference in the world in the election outcome. When it comes to name recognition and the ability to raise money, many would suggest that Democrats like Biden and O'Rourke were stronger challengers than were David Alameel and Wendy Davis. But the perception of timing and opportunity are the keys to attracting quality challengers to a campaign against an entrenched incumbent. The midterm of a relatively unpopular presidency convinced O'Rourke to challenge Cruz, and O'Rourke gave the incumbent senator a scare. The relative unpopularity of Trump attracted Joe Biden to the 2020 presidential race, and Biden did relatively well against Trump in Texas. More popular incumbents like Abbott and Cornyn were able to weather the storms of 2018 and 2020 in Texas, but as we noticed before, they won with smaller vote margins in those years than in earlier years.

Unlike what some pundits had predicted, Texas did not turn blue or even purple in 2020. But, without a doubt, Texas is a paler shade of red now than in 2012 or 2014. Republicans will have to continue to field strong candidates to overcome the apparent drag that Donald Trump had on the ballot in Texas. The tide to keep Texas red will be difficult, because the percentage of registered voters who identify as Moderates is increasing and issues that Texas will have to continue to contend with like border security and immigration are becoming politicized. Texas Democrats are certainly using the changing political environment and diverse issues on the table to their advantage by challenging the choices made by state leaders who are all Republican.

CHAPTER 7

Race and Social Justice in Texas Politics

There's a great awakening... like I've never seen before, and [it] will end up leading to systemic change in our country.
—Houston Police Chief Art Acevedo, 2020[1]

R EPUBLICANS HAVE A RACE problem. Two reasons explain this dilemma. First, since the 1960s, the party has become Whiter (and more male). In 2019, Whites made up roughly eight-in-ten of nationally registered Republicans. That number is larger among state-level elected officials.[2] Consequently, in an ever-diversifying nation, the GOP is a racially homogenous group. This is also true in Texas (81% of the party is White). Second, public confidence in the party's ability to address race relations is (and has been) low. This is not "accidental, vestigial, or comical."[3] It is a perception born from the last half-century of Republican Party officials using "racial pandering to win support from white voters."[4] From the "Southern strategy" to Donald Trump, the party has built a reputation with the public that can be safely described as "reactionary" when it comes to race in America.

In Texas, the 2020 landscape was at its most competitive in communities growing with racial diversity and urbanization outside city centers. The change occurred during the 2018 and 2020 election cycles as Texas became the center of debates about the border wall, immigration, protests during the national anthem, confederate monuments, Black Lives Matter, and #DefundthePolice as racial and ethnic wedge issues in Texas. This chapter will analyze how these contemporary wedge issues impacted Texas voter opinions on the major political parties, candidates for office, and cultural and social changes.

Abstracting racial issues has become a time-honored appeal for the GOP. Lee Atwater—campaign manager for Texan George H. W. Bush in 1988— articulated this approach during an infamous interview: "You start out in 1954 by saying, 'Nigger, nigger, nigger.' By 1968 you can't say 'nigger'—that hurts you, backfires. So you say stuff like, uh, forced busing, states' rights, and all that stuff, and you're getting so abstract. Now, you're talking about cutting taxes, and all these things you're talking about are totally economic things and a byproduct of them is, Blacks get hurt worse than whites. . . . 'We want to cut this,' is much more abstract than even the busing thing, uh, and a hell of a lot more abstract than 'Nigger, nigger.'"[5] In his statement, Atwater mentioned forced busing and states' rights. Over the proceeding decades, other issues included affirmative action,[6] housing integration,[7] welfare reform,[8] and the "War on Drugs."[9] The consistent theme is that these issues were major concerns among White Texans.

According to Smith (1996), White working and middle-class voters in the 1980s resented the Democratic Party's close association with Blacks and other racial minorities. So much so that national Democrats were perceived as the party of the "other."[10] Texas Republicans courted agitated Southern Whites by espousing conservative racial policies and weakening its historical ties to Black (and Brown) causes. This Southern strategy was successful in Texas because it subtly racialized wedge political issues.

The Politics of Law and Order

For the better part of sixty years, the Republican Party has staked its reputation on being decisive advocates for "law and order."[11] In the 1960s, Republican candidates were vocal proponents for a larger, more stringent police force, as well as increasing federal spending for crime control, especially in urban centers. By the 1990s, with the war on drugs in full effect, conservatives aimed to strengthen (and lengthen) criminal sentencing and bolster law enforcement. Today's conservatives consistently couch border security (that is, "illegal immigration"), Black Lives Matter protests, and #DefundthePolice, with a "law and order" frame.

Republicans are apt to emphasize crime while campaigning for office because they are attempting to set the issue agenda.[12] This allows the party and its candidates to "fix voter attention on issues where they are perceived as strong and their opponents are perceived as weak," as this focus increases their chance for electoral success.[13] This longstanding party posture has resulted in widespread public confidence in the party to handle crime. In recent years, the party has embraced a Blue Lives Matter attitude, a stance in contrast with organizations like Black Lives Matter. This counter attitude is framed to align Republicans with the police and law and order, while Democrats stand by BLM, the looters, anti-police activists, and disorder. The prevailing policy issue (and hashtag movement) of summer 2020 gave traction to a conflict of visions on public safety, allowing Republicans in Texas to go on the offensive and tread familiar political terrain after the George Floyd protests became international news.

Black Lives Matter

The Black Lives Matter movement's vocal lamentations of White supremacy and racism within the criminal justice system was immediately polarizing. Early public opinion polling revealed a racial (and partisan) divide between Blacks and Whites. A Pew Research poll found that 65 percent of Blacks (compared with 40% of Whites) supported Black Lives Matter.[14] A September 2016 CNN/ORC Poll showed 59 percent of Democrats had a favorable opinion of BLM, compared with just 20 percent of Republicans.

By the summer of 2020, these racial and partisan lines were even more distinct in Texas. Nearly half of White Texans had an unfavorable view of the movement, while 78 percent of Black Texans held a favorable opinion. Forty-eight percent of Latinos were favorable toward BLM. Asian Texans were more ambivalent; 36 percent held a neutral position, while 39 percent were favorable. And while more than 70 percent of Texas Democrats were favorable, an identical number of Republicans were *unfavorable* (66%). Independents were equally favorable and unfavorable.

Once the movement became an international phenomenon, Black Lives Matter's popularity among Black Americans could only be matched by the enmity conservatives and supporters of law enforcement felt toward it. The movement was quickly characterized as "anti-police," and blamed for attacks against police officers. Defensive phrases like "All Lives Matter" and "Blue Lives Matter" were created as countermovements.

Advocates using the police to set a wedge decried BLM protests as promoting looting and violence. They characterized these peaceful demonstrations as counterproductive and an "undermining" of "compelling" grievances. To be clear, in communities where protests have occurred, tension between officers and protesters, as well as the overwhelming angst and anger of participants, has resulted in violent clashes. In Ferguson, Missouri, after Mike Brown's murder, looters destroyed local businesses, and similar looting occurred in Baltimore, Baton Rouge, Seattle, Portland, and Minneapolis. That said, nonviolent activism was the prevailing behavior of the protestors, with marches, sit-ins, die-ins, speeches, and human blockades.[15] Importantly, in Texas these protests have not (yet) descended into violent conflict.

But the enduring media images of nighttime violence were hard to ignore. And media fascination with this behavior, particularly conservative media like Fox News, meant viewers would have daily exposure to what appeared to be uncontrolled anarchy. For an aging audience with long memories, it all harkened back to the days of the Watts riots in 1965 or the urban riots immediately after the assassination of Martin Luther King Jr. The coverage appeared as a sort of time-warp to a deadly and divisive time. It felt again like 1968, what journalist Jules Witcover called, "The year the dream died."[16] There was a sense, particularly among White Americans watching the urban riots unfold on television, of lawlessness and danger to the point viewers felt like public safety was under threat.

#Defund the Police

In the throes of a competitive battle for control of the Texas State Legislature and the White House, the Texas Freedom Caucus campaigned on "public safety matters." The message was not subtle in excoriating the "wrong direction" of public safety in Texas. Republican state representative Matt Schaefer stood in front of the city of Austin police headquarters and claimed it looked like "a place that's been under attack." The assailants—he argued—were those who advocated for defunding the police. The ad was clearly released to excite conservative Republicans in time for early voting in Texas. Embedded within its critiques of defunding the police is a call-to-arms by Schaefer to "stand up" for law enforcement and public safety. It ends with members of the Freedom Caucus repeatedly asserting that "public safety matters"—and vowing to "fight all efforts to defund the police."

Texans were primed to react to an issue-based argument that centered on race and violence in society. In El Paso, a gunman targeted Latino shoppers in a mass shooting at a Walmart in 2019 specifically because of their perceived Mexican heritage. The tragic memory of three murders of Black men and women in Texas—Sandra Bland, Botham Jean, and Atatiana Jefferson by police officers between 2015 and 2019 continued to motivate calls for police reform in the Black community. The public protests in Texas calling for justice in the killing of Houston-born George Floyd created a bridge for local communities to advocate for more robust reforms. The recency of these events, and the murder of Breonna Taylor in Louisville, added expedience to the calls for police abolitionism.

Advocacy for the idea of police abolitionism has its roots in academic and activist circles. W. E. B. DuBois and Walter Benjamin are credited with developing the foundations of police abolitionism, while later scholars like Amna Akbar, Alex Vitale, Angela Davis, and Ruth Wilson Gilmore refined it to what it is today. Their articulation of police abolitionism argues that the system of policing is needless and oppressive. An early iteration of the initiative promoted the need to shift from state-based policing to community-based policing, but proponents have since embraced the more radical approach of dismantling the institution altogether. This can be done—advocates argue—by reallocating tax dollars spent on law enforcement and investing in social programs and public services that address the root causes of crime (such as poverty). The murders of Floyd and Taylor breathed life into policy considerations that embrace principles of police abolitionism. It became a full-fledged policy prescription by academics, activists, allies, and notably, policymakers.

In the summer of 2020, the Minneapolis City Council unanimously approved a proposal to eliminate the city's police department. It was a radical step that has since been moderated, but a verifiable indication that progressive-led cities would be open to adopting the once-fringe precepts of police abolitionism. At the same time, Fort Worth was already scheduled to vote on a local bond initiative to extend the sales tax that provides more than $85 million to the police department's budget. The measure was targeted by advocates of #DefundthePolice as a test run in a more conservative area. For context, this was during the heat of the George Floyd protests when the country's moral indignation was at its peak. It was also merely a year since a Fort Worth officer killed a Black woman named Atatiana Jefferson. The synergy was evident. There was no time like the present to convince voters of their cause.

Pamela Young, community organizer with United Fort Worth, told a local publication, *The Eagle*, that extending funds was not really preventing crime nor violence. In fact, she argued, "It's only responding to crime and many times perpetuating violence, especially in Black and brown impoverished neighborhoods." She added, "This enhances SWAT teams, it goes into policing our schools, it goes to increase surveillance in our communities."[17] Her statement is at the core of the defund activists' argument. Ultimately, the extension was overwhelmingly approved by 64 percent of Fort Worth voters, signifying the public's less than voracious appetite for embracing the defund strategy.

Fort Worth was only one of several proxy wars on the issue of defunding the police in mid-2020. Two other major Texas cities—Austin and Dallas—were also the scene of political fights. Later that summer, the Austin City Council approved the city's budget for fiscal year 2020–2021, which included a $150 million shift in funds away from the Austin Police Department. The "shift" only cut about $20 million from the police budget, while the bulk redirected certain functions away from the police department to civilian-controlled public safety programs. Yet, it sparked a reaction across the state.

To be clear, unlike Fort Worth, the city of Austin has a progressive reputation, making it fertile ground to advance the cause of defund strategies without alienating the local population. But Austin's political standing (it is, after all, the seat of government for the state of Texas) also made it a prime target for a Republican backlash and gave the state GOP an opening to identify a bogeyman and once again weaponize "law and order."

Governor Abbott spoke out against the defund policy agenda. He said, "Defunding and disrespecting police is the worst possible policy a municipality or a state could adopt."[18] Characterizing anything but the status quo to be disrespectful was a familiar pivot. This allowed the governor and the state Republican Party to feign and foment outrage. To formalize the issue within the election, Governor Abbott introduced a "Texas Backs the Blue Pledge" for all Texas candidates in the 2020 November election to sign. It was a litmus test designed to corner Democrats, knowing that few, if any, would sign it.

The governor made public safety a central part of the party's agenda in the next state legislative session in 2021. Abbott explored legislation that would force the comptroller not to release local sales tax monies to any city that "defunds the police." The governor also threatened that the state would take over the Austin Police Department, controlling its operations and budget decisions, at the city's expense.

Collectively, these efforts were enough to deter Dallas public officials from parroting Austin. Initially, city officials voted to cut about $7 million from the police overtime budget. Instead, that money would be used to hire civilian police, improve traffic safety, build better street lighting, bike lanes, and pay for affordable housing and cultural programs. Council members were adamant that their vote was not tantamount to defunding the police. But that is not how the governor saw things, and just as he did with Austin, he called out the Dallas City Council until officials later amended their intentions and increased the police budget. Again, the "bully pulpit" was used to immense success.

Once the national discussion shifted from the protests as response to the murder of George Floyd to "defund the police," old racial (and partisan) fault lines became more apparent in our statewide polling. While conservative Whites were never fully supportive of the BLM protests, they were less antagonistic toward them when framed as a response to the egregious killing of Floyd. Conservative elites towed a line of remorse and were openly critical of the police officers involved in the incident. This tact changed once the coverage of the protests began to highlight nighttime rioting and looting in American cities. Republican responses to these images elicited a familiar phrase, that is, law and order. Once the politics of law and order became the central issue, the Republican Party—taking its cues from Donald Trump—reimagined the protests as an assault on public safety and law enforcement itself.

By October of 2020, Republican candidates campaigned against #DefundthePolice in two important ways. First, they argued that it was an assault on law enforcement; and second, they insisted that it threatened public safety. It was a politically savvy approach because of its framing. Despite the narrative bandied about in the national press, the local police are still an overwhelmingly trusted institution. Between 2018–2020, when asked how "warmly" they feel toward specific groups, the local police were consistently top-rated by Texans. This suggests that there was little (if any) appetite for perceived slights against police officers, especially those of a critical nature. An even more powerful trigger for the public is the idea that their own safety is imperiled. Linking #DefundthePolice with fewer police officers on the streets and an increase in "violence and fear" was intuitive.

The aggressive campaign against police abolitionism by Governor Abbott and Republicans was no coincidence. Texans had an overwhelmingly negative opinion of the phrase "defund the police." By fall 2020, the phrase was toxic in Texas. An overwhelming majority of Texans opposed the idea. And it was not close. Sixty percent of Texans expressed opposition to "defunding the police."

Strong opposition could be found across racial groups, parties, and genders. Though, as one might expect, Black respondents were more receptive to the idea. What is unmistakable (and more to the point) is the overwhelming opposition among key voting constituencies in Texas, namely White women (68%), and Independents (57%). These are the voters the Republican Party was targeting with its message against defunding the police.

The linearity between age and support (or opposition) to the "defund" initiative is quite striking. A majority (51%) of eighteen-to-twenty-four-year old's support the idea, but this sentiment consistently diminishes with age.

Progressive activists lamented Barack Obama's critique that "snappy slogans" like "Defund the Police" are not particularly helpful for the movement. The former president had clearly surmised the political viability of the phrase. Regardless of how one feels about the slogan and the substance behind it, our data suggest Obama was correct about the slogan weighing down a policy agenda that would otherwise earn more public support.

When asked about the agenda behind the slogan, there is significantly more support (or at the least less antagonism) among registered Texans. Overall public opposition dropped by 14 percent when voters were asked about "cutting some funding from police departments to increase spending on social services in your community" in place of "defunding the police." Resistance to defunding the police appears to have shifted toward support for cutting some funding and reallocating it. This is also true across partisan affiliation. The biggest jump in support was among Democrats (22%), followed by Independents. Republicans barely budged on level of support, but their decline in opposition is notable.

From a purely cynical point of view, one could argue that conservative outrage (at the elite level) was solely a matter of political theater. With the upcoming election, Republicans needed the national (and statewide) conversation to shift from the COVID-19 crisis and healthcare (two issues that were politically beneficial for Democrats) to something within their wheelhouse. And touting "law and order" has long been associated with GOP success. Because the protests were not going away, and neither the Black Lives Matter movement, nor Democratic candidates, would cede ground for media coverage, national and statewide Republicans needed to take the offensive. They would tie BLM, national anthem protests, and "Defund the Police" as threats in a culture war—pitting urban Democratic cities against the suburbs and rural communities.

The Suburbs and the Urban-Rural Divide

Nationally, much had been written about the Trump-led Republican Party bleeding support in the suburbs. This was especially the case among White, suburban women. For instance, in June 2020, a *New York Times*/Siena poll showed most Americans disapproved of Trump's job on race (61%). Significantly, 65 percent of women disapproved of how Trump was handling race relations. When asked about Trump's handling of the protests after the death of George Floyd, 62 percent disapproved (including 64% of women). Amid a consequential election year, Republicans were desperate to change their fortunes here. The tricky part was figuring out how to do so.

The urban-rural divide in Texas necessarily made political competition within suburban communities the setting where the state became a battleground. In a red-blue state scheme, the suburbs were the "purple" swing states. The Republican strategy to campaign against "Defund the Police" and tie their Democratic opponents to the slogan was especially resonant in these politically important communities (and races). And fortunately for the party, given the overwhelming unpopularity of the slogan, "Defund the Police" came to it like manna from heaven.

Several U.S. House seats were decided by suburban communities, and the results suggest that there was an edginess about the "defund" idea. Republican candidates appealed to voters in two ways. First, they warned that defunding the police would spike crime rates. This was a direct appeal to those White suburban women who had traditionally been receptive to the message. For decades, certainly since the 1970s, punitive criminal justice measures were adopted across the country on the strength of widespread fear of violent criminals. In New York City, for instance, a political regime change led by Republican mayor Rudolph Giuliani ushered in an era of decidedly aggressive policing strategies. He targeted neighborhood "disorder" as the principal culprit of spiking violent crime rates and low morale. As such, "disorder policing" was adopted to aggressively target lower-level offenses and proponents credited it with the drop in crime during the 1990s. Once deemed successful, this approach was adopted throughout the nation, including Texas. This policy approach worked to assuage rural and suburban voters who expected politicians to do something (and be tough) about crime. GOP 2020 campaign ads deftly harkened back to the old playbook.

Political science research observes that when policies have a strong racial component, they can incite feelings of racial consciousness and influence voting behavior.[19] Consequently, the "perception of racial threat is critical in provoking negative reactions to Black candidates among whites."[20] The racial identity of Candace Valenzuela and Colin Allred (especially in contrast to their opponents) may have made it easier for their opponents Beth Van Duyne and Genevieve Collins to (mis)characterize their positions on defunding the police. The contrast between the candidates also made it easier to trigger White (and Black) voter group consciousness and, in this climate, sour otherwise receptive White, moderate voters to the prospect of voting for candidates of color.

Beth Van Duyne stood in symbolic contrast to her Democratic opponent, Candace Valenzuela. A former Carrollton-Farmers Branch school board member, and progressive mother of two, Valenzuela—who is a Black Latina—was not a prototypical candidate in TX-24. She unabashedly ran on her racial identity, touting the need for "representation" in Congress, as well as highlighting her working-class background. Valenzuela publicly opposed defunding the police but embraced aspects of the Black Lives Matter agenda. She called for a ban on chokeholds, an end to no-knock warrants, and an emphasis on deescalation training. It was enough of an association that Van Duyne could tie her to the defund movement.

During the 2020 cycle, flanked by a group of police officers, Beth Van Duyne ran an ad called "No Police, No Peace." Using stock footage of police officers under duress, the candidate opined: "Four years ago, five police officers were gunned down in downtown Dallas, inspired by the same anti-police rhetoric we see today. Unfortunately, my opponent Candace Valenzuela sides with radicals to defund the police and end cash bail, releasing criminals back on the streets." The pitch was unmistakable: elect my Democratic opponent and the criminals will run amok. The campaign message aired in a district where the two female candidates were running in an open election to replace Republican Kenny Marchant (R).

The TX-32 race between freshman Democrat Colin Allred and Republican businesswoman Genevieve Collins was projected to be a competitive election. A former linebacker for the Tennessee Titans and practicing civil rights attorney, Colin Allred won his seat in the Democratic wave of 2018 by defeating Representative Pete Sessions. Collins, like Van Duyne, attempted to tie her Democratic opponent to the defund the police policy by weaponizing Allred's "silence" on defund the police to make political hay. The ad, "Allred Silent on Defunding Police," used riot footage, explicitly designed to prime the audience to not only fear for their safety but also resent leaders who allowed the violence to flourish. The theme was Congressman Allred's avoidance of the issue. In their televised debate, Allred charged his opponent with demagoguery, pitting citizens against one another.

The most explicit use of racial politics came later in the Allred-Collins race, in a particularly nasty dustup between the candidates over a campaign mailer sent out by Collins that, Allred argued, deliberately darkened his skin tone. The mailer was a two-sided leaflet. With Collins brightly lit on one side, the language reads: "Genevieve Collins will always stand with our police officers and first responders." It also included a seal of endorsement from the Dallas Police Association. On the other side, Allred is darkly lit, transposed next to "Antifa" protesters, with the language: "Colin Allred voted to restrict funding of the police and put our families at risk." This was an explicitly racialized appeal and Collins was not shy about it.

These examples are important because previous research suggests that the contrasting racial identities of each candidate could have played a factor in a voter's preference. The most prominent voices of both Black Lives Matter and the defund movement have been Black. Their cause (criminal justice reform) is explicitly racial and activities (summer protests) have elicited strong, racially distinct reactions. Everything about the issue of defunding the police—particularly as a proxy for "law and order"—makes race a salient and triggering factor.

We cannot argue for certain that racial identity was the determining factor in either race. After all, the decision was split, Van Duyne won by three points, and Allred won by six. That said, if we rely on Mendelberg's theory on the "norms of racial equality," a case can be made that Van Duyne succeeded where Collins failed because she never crossed the threshold of implicit racial appeals during the campaign. Voters in the DFW metroplex followed a pattern that public beliefs in racial egalitarianism constrain the nature of campaigns. These norms create contradictory conditions for parties that must adhere to norms of racial equality, while also dealing with a party system that is based on the cleavage of race. For instance, campaigns must avoid violating racial equality, but face incentives to (in the Republicans' case) mobilize racially reactionary White voters. On the flip side, White voters have their own contradictory conditions. While they wish to advance racial equality, there is a simmering resentment toward "identity politics," which is seen as special attention given to minorities.

When Collins distributed that mailer, she crossed a norm, making explicit an appeal that required implicit priming, and triggering a possible backlash. This, in addition to the obvious incumbency advantage of Allred, could be a reasonable explanation about why she failed to cash-in on an anti-defund strategy that worked for Van Duyne.

Arguably, immigration is an issue exempt from Mendelberg's theory. Explicit anti-immigration messages and the criminalization of immigrants have produced some of the most contentious political images in modern political history. Furthermore, "law and order" was not a phrase strictly reserved for social protests on criminal justice reform. Conservatives would also employ it to describe their views on immigration at the southern border.

The Many Fronts of Immigration

The politics of immigration was a bit of a hydra in 2018. First, there was the question of the border wall. A signature promise of the Trump campaign in 2016 was to build a wall along the U.S.-Mexico border. By early 2018, the president was determined to make-good on this pledge, even if it meant forcing a shutdown of the federal government. Second, the Trump administration would weather widespread criticism for its family separation policy in the summer of 2018. Media coverage of young children (who had been separated from their parents once apprehended at the border) detained in facilities with chain-link fencing and bare floors, ignited national indignation. And while Republicans supported the administration's "zero tolerance" approach, it managed to further alienate Democrats and Independents. Third, the president made the issue of turning back Central American migrant "caravans" a rallying opportunity for Republicans, just in time for the midterm election. Indeed, the politics of immigration in 2018—both nationally and in Texas—were filtered (and framed) through the Twitter feed of the man in the Oval Office. He forced the country to confront its policies on immigration and furthered the polarization (and calcification) of attitudes on the subject.

"CRimmigration"

Republicans have long framed *illegal* immigration as a "law and order" issue. In 2018, conservative historian Victor Davis Hanson wrote, "Once someone makes a decision to enter a country illegally—his first decision as an incoming alien—and thus breaks a U.S. law with impunity, then most subsequent decisions are naturally shaped by the idea of exemption."[21] Montana's Republican governor signed a law banning "sanctuary cities" in part because "we are a nation of laws, and immigration laws will be enforced in Montana."[22] These are the intellectual foundations of a message that argues that coming to the United States illegally is a crime in and of itself—and an affront to our "nation of laws."

But arguments against undocumented immigrants do not end at illegal border crossings. Under the leadership of Donald Trump, conservatives regularly rhetorically wed immigrants with *criminality*. Trump's opening salvo against Mexican immigrants who "bring drugs" and are "rapists" set the tone. During the 2018 midterm cycle, Republicans linked immigrants to crime with images of street gangs (like MS-13) committing "terrible crimes, horrific crimes"[23]—namely against American citizens like Kathryn Steinle—who was murdered by Juan Francisco Lopez-Sanchez, a Mexican national with seven felony convictions and who had been deported five times but had returned to the United States. Steinle's killing was used to advance unsubstantiated claims that undocumented immigrants kill thousands of Americans a year and harsher anti-immigration laws that would be tough on "criminal aliens." The Trump administration's threat of nationwide Immigration and Customs Enforcement (ICE) raids were partially predicated on this messaging.

Legal scholar Julie Stumpf coined the phrase "CRimmigration" to describe the combining of criminal law and immigration law. Since the Reagan era, immigration laws have changed for immigrants who are accused of crimes. By design, it has become harder for them to seek justice and maintain their immigration status. Justification for altering these laws has earned support on both sides of the aisle, but in recent years, Republicans have framed getting tougher on immigrants as a means toward maintaining law and order.

Discussion and Conclusion

Something is happening in Texas. The battles for descriptive representation are diffuse across multiple races and ethnicities. Each change will generate new perspectives and may have a profound impact on Texan attitudes on racial wedge issues (and their political implications). The marvel of shifting racial and ethnic demographics in Texas is powering breathless political forecasting. National talk of a "blue shift" has been happening for the better part of a decade. Some speculators claim that migration from progressive states like California and New York is the reason that Texas will be competitive (since 2008, about seven hundred thousand California expats have moved to Texas). But the reality is that Texas's conservative, White plurality is aging, while younger Texans of color (specifically Latinos) will become a larger plurality as the decades proceed, is even more of a pronounced red flag for Republicans. We believe the urbanization of Texas and the increased presence of Latino voters is key to understanding the state's electoral future. It also explains why racial politics and attitudes in Texas appear so clearly delineated along racial and ethnic lines.

Between 1990 and 2018, a dual shift in racial and ethnic populations has occurred. The White (non-Hispanic) population has declined 19 percent, while Latinos (of any race) has increased by 15 percent. In raw numbers, there were a little more than four million Latino Texans after the 1990 national census. By 2019, census estimates place that population at more than ten million.

The population growth in Texas is mostly happening in the major metropolitan areas. According to a study commissioned by the Texas Demographic Center, the Lone Star State has experienced a 15 percent population growth between 2010 and 2019. In that same time, the state has welcomed a net 1.1 million new residents through domestic migration, plus another eight hundred thousand or so in international migration. Voter registration increased by about 2.3 million during the same time. Of the 254 counties in Texas, ten witnessed population spikes between one hundred to six hundred thousand people. Those ten counties were Denton, Collin, Tarrant, Dallas, Williamson, Travis, Bexar, Montgomery, Harris, and Fort Bend. These were also already ten of the most populous counties in the state.[24]

To be clear, growing metro areas and shrinking rural communities are not necessarily a harbinger of doom for Republicans in Texas. In fact, contrary to conventional wisdom, we find that Republicans are quite competitive in

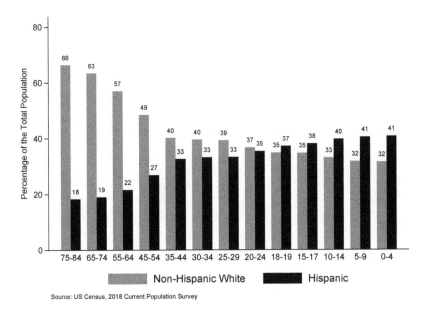

Source: US Census, 2018 Current Population Survey

Figure 7.1 Relative Ethnoracial Composition by Age in Texas 2018
(U.S. Census Bureau)

Texas metro areas like Dallas–Fort Worth and Houston. The issue is that the populations that are growing (or migrating) are younger (and thus more apt to highly influence future elections) and more Democratic, while Republican voters are older (and thus more likely to lose influence in future elections). For instance, examining the relative ethnoracial composition by age in Texas (as of 2018), reveals that the Latino population outnumbers non-Hispanic Whites at around eighteen years of age and younger (figure 7.1). And theoretically, these are folks who will increase as a percentage of the voting population for many elections to come. Conversely, while non-Hispanic Whites are dominant among older Texans, the facts of life suggest that these voters will not be participating in as many future elections.

CHAPTER 8

Selective Media Exposure and Political Attitudes

We're not even arguing from the same reality right now. So, if we can agree on facts, then I believe we can start building trust.
—Matthew McConaughey[1]

TEXANS WATCHING THE NEWS might notice that their representatives are only appearing on certain television networks. Increasingly, a one-stop-shop of elite media appearances from both parties is disappearing.[2] Sure, Sunday morning talk shows like "Meet the Press" still exist to platform "both sides" of a topical political dispute. But their cultural cachet is largely within the province of the "Acela corridor," an echo chamber in its own right, and hardly reaching (or influencing) many Texans. Instead, while New York City serves as the primary hub for traditional media outlets, what's closer to home for many Texans—especially conservatives—is the dominating presence of alternative media headquartered within the state. Texas houses national broadcast networks like Infowars, Newsmax TV, and The Blaze. It is also home to widely read conservative websites like Townhall.com, RedState, Hot Air, and PJ Media—all owned by Irving-based Salem Communications.

Texas's long tradition of fostering political news dates to H. L. Hunt, Sid Richardson, Clint Murchison, and Hugh Roy Cullen. These four wealthy oil men in the mid-twentieth century financed print, radio, and television shows programmed with anti-labor, anti-government, White supremacist, anti-Semitic, and anti-communist messaging. They channeled "tens of millions of dollars into new conservative causes, bankrolling everything from mainstream Republican think tanks to Senator Joe McCarthy's red-baiting campaigns of the 1950's to extremist groups; later, oil money helped bankroll

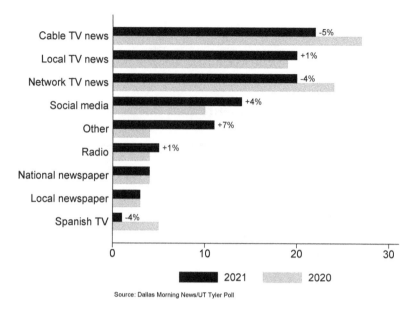

Figure 8.1 Primary News Sources among Texans, 2020 and 2021

the rise of the religious right."[3] That said, perhaps the greatest difference between then and 2020 is the broader public's (and the political elites') appetite for these hyperpartisan media platforms.

Our first step is to take a broad view of where Texans are getting their news and how this shifted between 2020 and 2021 (figure 8.1). Cable news outlets that produce news content twenty-four hours a day are the most common source, but this audience is only slightly higher than those who rely most on local television news. When we aggregate all responses, by the year the survey was taken, we see some meaningful shifts. Voters are relying less on cable television news and the national networks for their information. In turn, after the 2020 election, voters began to turn primarily to social media or indicate they choose other news outlets entirely.

The onslaught of information from nationally based news outlets was overwhelming. If an individual watched CNN, Fox News, or MSNBC in 2020, they were subjected to incessant countdowns to the next election day, and running tallies of coronavirus infections and then national deaths. These images reflected moments that defined the time, but also pushed some viewers

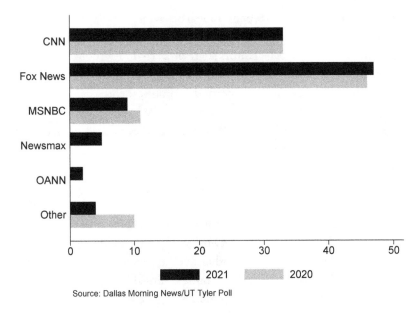

Source: Dallas Morning News/UT Tyler Poll

Figure 8.2 Station Preference among Texas's Cable News Audience, 2020 and 2021

away. Concurrent with this shift was the expansion of new right-wing news outlets like One American News Network and Newsmax that used coverage of the 2020 election to attract conservative viewers. In 2021, we diversified the set of available alternatives to respondents who said they watched cable news to include the two most popular new outlets (Newsmax and OANN). Figure 8.2 shows how station viewership varied among voters who primarily got their news from cable television. A comparison of primary viewership of 2021 to 2020 shows these new channels did not greatly fragment loyalty to Fox News among Texans. The decrease in the other channel response suggests that some of these voters were early viewers of the nascent networks. Another contrast that may show the growing importance of these information sources is the overall decline in cable news as a leading source of news and the rise of social media. Survey respondents often explained that they used social media to watch clips that were produced by Newsmax on YouTube.

Elected leaders from Texas have been integral to this increase in appetite for hyperpartisan media. In many ways, they help to drive differing media diets. For example, in a study conducted from January 2015 to July 2017, Pew

Research Analysis found that congressional behavior on social media is linked to partisan considerations. It found that "partisan and ideological divides shape which news outlets legislators share links to on Facebook."[4] Citizens' political opinions, decisions, and political efficacy are greatly influenced by polarized political environments created by political elites.[5] An East Texas constituent may regularly tune into Newsmax TV because he knows that is where his congressman will appear. When the congressman is not on the network the constituent is likely to be affected by the hyperpartisan information stream of that network.

Partisan media permeates a polarized public because audiences choose likeminded sources to bolster their preconceptions and solidify opinions.[6] Reasoned deliberation over the issues has become a casualty of selective media exposure, allowing our social networks to become increasingly homogenous, and antagonism toward the "other side" to pervade our everyday lives.[7] Increasingly, a holistic polarization among politically engaged citizens has normalized. That is, political polarization has made way for cultural and social polarization too, the sort of divide that has only worsened many interpersonal relationships between Democrats and Republicans.[8] The relationship between our polarized citizenry and selective media exposure is complex, but conventional wisdom agrees that there is an existing relationship between media choice and partisanship.[9] We too find evidence of this relationship.

Our surveys of Texans between 2020 and 2021 comport with national figures. In Texas, Democratic voters have a more diversified media diet, with sizable percentages choosing network news (27%), local news (17%), CNN (15%), Fox News (9%), and MSNBC (5%). Meanwhile, Republicans leaned more heavily toward one source: Fox News. Nearly one-in-four Republicans primarily get their news from Fox News, 20 percent from network news, and another 20 percent from local news networks. These numbers look strikingly like national Pew Research findings, where Democrats identified at least five sources of television news they trust (CNN, NBC News, ABC News, CBS News, and PBS), while Republicans overwhelmingly chose one (Fox News).[10] In the months where Fox News viewership among Republicans dipped, the choice of tuning into alternative new sources increased.

These comparisons bear the point that every citizen does not share the same media diet. Opinions on a myriad of salient political issues in Texas—from attitudes on COVID-19 to topical racial and ethnic concerns—are highly correlated with selective media exposure. In this chapter, we define how

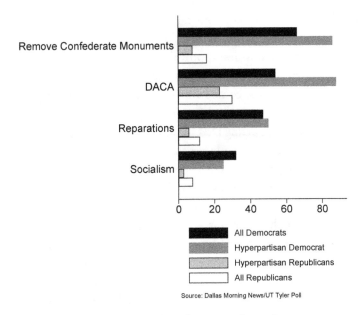

Figure 8.3 Support for Policies, by Selective Media Preference, 2019–2020

attitudes relate to partisan media exposure and what kinds of people are affected by this relationship. We are interested in probing three types of groups of individuals who consume partisan media: hyperpartisans, cross-cutters, and odd-partisans. These groups have the potential to explain whether entertainment had any effect on an individual's attitudes on salient political issues in Texas. Our interviews with Texans across the state allow us to investigate the characteristics of these groups in 2020 and 2021, because we asked the same set of questions about media consumption in those surveys.

Hyperpartisans

Some individuals selectively consume likeminded media, which increases the likelihood they will become hyperpartisans (figure 8.3).[11] For instance, based on national polling data from the past decade, we expect hyperpartisan Republicans to solely use cable news sources like Fox News. Conversely, we assume hyperpartisan Democrats primarily watch MSNBC.

Hyperpartisans earn the label by being the most ideologically extreme and consistently partisan on salient political issues.[12] Both hyperpartisan Democrats and Republicans differ from their fellow party members overall. Here, we examined four salient issues: approval for socialism, the Deferred Action for Childhood Arrivals (DACA) program, reparations for descendants of African slaves, and removal of confederate monuments from public spaces. We see hyperpartisan Democrats exhibit higher approval for removing confederate monuments and supporting DACA. Furthermore, as expected, hyperpartisan Republicans are consistently less supportive on all four of these issues.

These results are partially a consequence of partisan media sources promoting what Cass Sunstein calls "biased assimilation" and "crippled epistemology."[13] Both concepts describe individuals irrationally ignoring and dismissing evidence that does not agree with their predispositions and bolstering agreeable findings from likeminded sources.[14] In turn, hyperpartisans are more apt to embrace social and political networks where disagreement is least likely and unambiguous political messages are crafted.[15]

During the summer of 2020, hyperpartisans held the starkest views on the coronavirus crisis and racial issues in Texas. Republicans who solely consume Fox News were consistently the most skeptical of the COVID-19 crisis and the most antagonistic group toward Black Lives Matter, the protests during the national anthem, and #DefundthePolice. Democratic hyperpartisans were the most concerned about the virus and the biggest supporters of Black Lives Matter, the protests during the national anthem, and #DefundthePolice.

Cross Cutters

Not every Texan is hyperpartisan. Some consumers diversify their media consumption.[16] We call them cross-cutters. They are Republicans who primarily watch MSNBC and read the *New York Times*. They are Democrats who listen to conservative talk radio and NPR. They are also Independents who show little media source favoritism. These consumers tend to be less ideologically extreme and more ambivalent on salient political issues.[17] As a result of their socially and politically heterogeneous networks, cross-cutters have a greater understanding of opposing rationales and closer relationships across lines of difference.[18]

Yet, at the heart of their behavior is avoidance. Cross-cutters do not aspire to risk their social relationships and ambivalence is but one tool to evade social conflict.[19] Huckfeldt, Johnson, and Sprague argue that individuals within politically diverse networks are less likely to have polarized attitudes, less interested in politics, and more ambivalent.[20] They are also less likely to vote, provide less civic group participation, and spend more time deciding for whom to vote. In terms of media habits, Levendusky finds that cross-cutters who view media sources as credible will moderate their opinions after exposure.[21]

Odd-Partisans

Odd-partisans, meanwhile, are partisans who exclusively prefer contrary (or counter-attitudinal) media.[22] Predictably, this is a diminutive group, thus its traits have received less scholarly attention. Stroud only found about 16 percent of her sample population fell within the criteria of odd-partisan.[23] Nevertheless, Levendusky requests more consideration of who opts into consuming counter-attitudinal media and why they do so.[24] We have some clues that might help us to draw a few conclusions. These partisans may have an ideological complexity and confliction that explores beyond partisan identification and labels.[25] Voters may simply hold complex and contradictory opinions, which may in turn inform their selectivity.[26] Attitude and issue certainty may also play a role, as more confident partisans will seek out counter-attitudinal media to refute their claims.[27] For our research, these findings render problematic conclusions. "Complexity" and "confliction" suggest ambivalence, which may compromise (or lessen) interest in politics. Conversely, strategic consumption of counter-attitudinal media should show *higher* interest. We will not (and do not) look to answer this quandary. Instead, we will exclusively spotlight the odd-partisans within our sample, drawing fewer generalizable conclusions, but providing a basic profile of this group's attitudes and compare them to hyperpartisans and cross-cutters.

Ideological Composition of Selective Media Groups

Ideological diversity among these groups is also prevalent.[28] Democratic hyperpartisans are more liberal-identifying (63%) than Democrats overall (49%), cross-cutters (56%), and odd-partisans (16%). Cross-cutting Democrats are the most likely to call themselves "moderate" or "middle of the road" (32%), and conservative identification is highest among odd-partisan Democrats (64%).

Republican hyperpartisans are—by a wide margin—more conservative (88%) than Republicans overall (71%), cross-cutters (23%), and odd-partisans (20%). Republican cross-cutters and odd-partisans are equally moderate-identifying (30%), and liberal-identifying (46% and 49%, respectively).

Selective Media Exposure and Attitudes on Covid-19

In the spring of 2020, Infowars provocateur Alex Jones organized rallies against government measures to control the spread of COVID-19. These demonstrations were held in state capitals across the country. In Austin, Texas, Jones's display of anti-government bravura was especially ostentatious, as he manned an armored vehicle and excoriated the lockdown through a giant megaphone. As protesters shouted, "Open Texas now!" Jones—as if on a float during a parade—cruised down Congress Avenue and bellowed, "America will reopen! Texas is leading the way!"

The voice of Infowars articulated a growing sentiment among conservatives across the country. At his capital protest, he shouted, "We're going to tell the globalists, 'we're not your slaves, we're not in your cult, and if you want war, you better believe you got war.'"[29] These references to slavery were a part of the Right's pushback against what they viewed as government control of individual liberty during the pandemic. Their demonstrations were deliberately unmasked, and protesters—who wielded banners that read, "Texas Will Not Take the Mark of the Beast (Vaccine Chip, ID2020)"—refused to socially distance.

By the time of these protests, popular Fox News host Sean Hannity had regularly compared COVID-19 to the "seasonal flu." Conservative talk radio host Rush Limbaugh called it the "common cold," claiming the coronavirus is far less lethal than the flu.[30] And President Donald Trump tweeted: "So last year 37,000 Americans died from the common Flu. It averages between 27,000 and 70,000 per year. Nothing is shut down; life & the economy go on. At this moment there are 546 confirmed cases of Coronavirus, with 22 deaths. Think about that!"

This holy trinity of prominent conservative voices was a potent force in shaping the attitudes of conservatives and Republicans on the coronavirus. Indeed, a March 2020 YouGov/Economist national poll found that while 74 percent of MSNBC viewers were worried about the virus, only 38 percent of Fox News viewers agreed. A Pew Research poll from the same period found similar results. A significant number of Fox News viewers believed that

Democrats were exaggerating the risks of the virus (44%), the media was exaggerating the risks (56%), and that COVID-19 was developed in a Chinese laboratory (31%).

Our data allude to a similar trend in Texas. In an April 2020 survey, we asked registered voters if they agreed or disagreed that "coronavirus is a major health threat." Around 10 percent of Fox News viewers disagreed with the statement. Initially, 10 percent seems like a diminutive figure (and should not be overstated), but when compared with MSNBC (2%) and CNN (1%) viewers, there was a significant gulf in opinion. Fox News viewers were also the least likely to agree (81% compared with MSNBC (95%) and CNN (96%).

In that same survey, when Texas voters were asked if the "threat of the coronavirus has been blown out of proportion," more than half of Fox News viewers agreed (52%), while a majority of MSNBC (66%) and CNN (63%) viewers *disagreed*. Media coverage of the virus explain these numbers. For example, Fox Business host Trish Regan delivered a blistering rebuke against media coverage of COVID-19, calling it a "coronavirus impeachment scam." She monologued: "The chorus of hate being leveled at the president is nearing a crescendo as Democrats blame him, and only him, for a virus that originated halfway around the world. This is yet another attempt to impeach the president. . . . Sadly, it seems they care very little for any of the destruction they are leaving in their wakes."[31] Regan was later fired from the network, but her sentiments, wedding views of the virus's severity with feelings toward Donald Trump, were clearly in line with Fox's audience.

Budak, Muddiman, and Stroud's analysis of cable news coronavirus coverage found "Fox News and MSNBC coronavirus coverage discussed partisans more than health experts." As for the disparity in opinion on the scale of the virus as a threat, "MSNBC described the virus using such words as 'crisis' and 'bad' more often than did Fox News and CNN." They noted that "popular cable news programs are presenting coronavirus information in ways that map onto party politics. Fox News and MSNBC present starkly different views of the virus."[32]

When analyzed through the prism of partisan identification and selective media exposure, the "major threat" results are not as distinct. All Democrats overall agreed that the coronavirus was a major threat (95%). The 5 percent dip came largely from odd-partisan Democrats who were less likely to agree (79%). Republicans overall were less in agreement on the threat question (85%), while hyperpartisan Republicans were not significantly different in their assessment (84%). Cross-cutter Republicans were slightly more likely to recognize the coronavirus as a major threat (90%) and odd-partisans were in complete agreement that there was a threat.

The effect of hyperpartisan media exposure on the question of whether the virus was blown out of proportion was clearer. Hyperpartisan Democrats (78%) were about 9 percent more likely than Democrats overall (69%) to disagree with that assessment. A majority of hyperpartisan Republicans (52% *agreed*, which was slightly more than Republicans overall (48%).

As testing became more readily available, the national conversation around the virus shifted to preventative and prescriptive measures. States shut down businesses, implemented mask mandates, and talk of vaccinations began. And once again, the veracity of information received (and its impact on audience attitudes) was dependent upon media source. On masks, scholars found "a troubling rate of misinformation, particularly from Fox News, where just over one in 10 sampled segments about mask-wearing suggested said it was unnecessary, even after the CDC released its guidelines."[33] Stanford's Cable News TV Analyzer reveals that during the spring of 2020, MSNBC viewers were more likely to hear "wear a mask" than the Fox News audience. But CNN viewers were likeliest to hear the phrase. This aligns with the previously mentioned study, which found that CNN mentioned healthcare officials more often than partisans.[34] It stands to reason that an invited epidemiologist on CNN would be more likely than a partisan commentator on MSNBC or Fox to mention the necessity of mask wearing.

By July 2020, the effects of selective media exposure appeared to have strengthened. Fox News viewers dropped in agreement to the statement that the coronavirus was a major threat (from 81% to 76%) and rose in disagreement (from 10% to 12%). This shift occurred while the virus death toll mounted, and the national infection rate steadily grew since April. In July 2020, 56 percent of Fox viewers believed the virus was blown out of proportion (compared with 52% in April). Viewers from other cable sources were overwhelmingly likely to see COVID-19 as a major threat and disagreed that it was blown out of proportion.

Mirroring how the crisis was framed, hyperpartisan Democrats were more likely to see the virus as a major threat than Democrats overall (98% to 92%), while about 72 percent of odd-partisan Democrats agreed (a drop in 7 points since April). Republicans overall fell in agreement on the threat question in July (from 85% to 82%), as did hyperpartisan Republicans (from 82% to 79%).

Democrats, overall, grew in disagreement from April (69%) to July (71%) on whether the virus was overblown, as did hyperpartisan Democrats (from 78% to 89%). Republicans overall did not move much on the question (49%), but hyperpartisan Republicans grew stronger in agreement over the four-month period (from 52% to 58%), again suggesting a media effect.

Selective Media Exposure and Attitudes on Race Issues

Selective media framing of racial issues varied in 2020. For instance, over on Fox News's "Tucker Carlson" program, viewers were met with headlines that characterized the Black Lives Matter protests as "mobs,"[35] while readers of the Far-Left website Media Matters lament the "Right-wing vilification" of the movement.[36] Fox News viewers were told that NFL players ought to "get off their knees and lead a constructive conversation on race,"[37] while readers of the *New York Times* read the headline, "The Law Is on the NFL Players' Side."[38] And then there was the issue of defunding the police. On the Right, the *Wall Street Journal* predicted a return of crime if the activists got their way. On the Left, countless headlines tried to explain what the slogan actually meant. A media siloed Republican was only going to hear or read the worst of the proposal, while a Democrat might have only read or heard about the best-case scenario.

Because of the extremely distinct nature of selective media and framing issues like Black Lives Matter, kneeling during the anthem, and defund the police, we found a few things consistent with our typology in Texas. First, as expected, hyperpartisan Democrats were significantly more favorable toward Black Lives Matter than other Democratic categories. Compared with all Democrats, this group was about 14 percent more favorable. Among Republicans, the effect of hyperpartisan selective media exposure was even stronger. Republicans who exclusively watch Fox News were about 17 percent more unfavorable toward Black Lives Matter than Republicans overall. And while neutrality among cross-cutting Republicans was the highest of any Republican category (35%), most of these voters held a favorable opinion of BLM.

Analysis of cable news coverage from June to November 2020 suggests that viewers of Fox News were more likely than CNN or MSNBC audiences to hear the word "protests" tied with "looting" throughout the summer of 2020. Interestingly, a similar assessment found that the words "protests" and "riot" were more likely to be mentioned on CNN during the early months of the summer, but during the period immediately after the Republican National

Convention—where the GOP spent a considerable amount of time decrying BLM protests—until Election Day, Fox News coverage spiked ahead of its competitors with this word association.

Second, hyperpartisan Democrats were more *ambivalent* on the right of athletes to kneel during the national anthem (89%) than Democrats overall (72%) and all other categories. These were confounding results. We did not expect such large percentages of neutrality among Democrats, perhaps suggesting that the framing of the kneeling issue (as disrespectful of service members) had a bipartisan impact (regardless of media source), at least among Texas Democrats. Results from our March 2021 Texas survey on a related issue shows that Texas Democrats are perhaps just more ambivalent on sports-related race matters than one might expect. When asked if sports teams should have to play the national anthem before games, 52 percent of Democrats overall answered in the affirmative. Conversely, hyperpartisan Democrats would have none of it. Sixty-four percent of these voters answered, "No, no requirement at all"; which is a fascinatingly mixed message from Democrats on these sports-related race questions. Things make more sense among Republicans. Hyperpartisans are most likely to oppose the right of athletes to kneel (77%), but ambivalence levels are identical among cross-cutters (64%) and odd-partisans (64%), as one might expect.

Third, Texas Democrats once again defied our expectations on the question of defunding the police. It is not hyperpartisan Democrats who showed the most support for the initiative. Instead, cross-cutting Democrats were most enthusiastic (42%). Republicans continued to meet our expectations on the defund issue. Hyperpartisans were the most opposed group (88%), cross-cutters were the most supportive (44%), and odd-partisans were the most neutral (42%).

For the most part, Texan attitudes of race issues—even filtered through a selective media lens—are like national trends. While Texans have unique experiences relating to some of the more controversial racial issues of the day (namely immigration), like much of the rest the country, most political matters have increasingly become nationalized, partisan battles. This makes it harder to distinguish the attitudes of a partisan in Texas from a partisan in New York. Where there are differences—such as Texas Democratic ambivalence toward kneeling during the national anthem—something again must be said for how much further right-of-center these voters are from the national Democratic electorate. Specific to their media choices, Texas has a Democratic bloc that consumes conservative media at relatively higher numbers than Democrats elsewhere. About 29 percent of Texas Democrats regularly watch Fox News. Nationally, that figure is around 6 percent.[39]

Texas Republican attitudes are predictable on these issues and are the byproduct of a nationalized political environment. In addition to the GOP's election year, rally-around-the-party leader effect—including full-throated support for Trump's political messages and defending against national media critiques of his performance—there is the added impact of the larger culture war, which serves as jet fuel for both issue *and* affective polarization. Partisan cueing from national Republican leaders on issues like the protests (and their so-called association with rioting and looting) has meant that even in places like Texas, where rioting and looting did not occur, GOP voters were able to form antagonistic attitudes toward protesters and "the Left" who back them.

Selective Media Exposure, Local and National Coverage, and Approval Ratings

Americans have clear opinions on local and national coverage. While national media outlets (be it print, television, or online) are considered more prestigious, garner far larger audiences, and enable personality-driven, audience devotion (particularly as it relates to cable news personalities), local outlets are more widely trusted.[40] Furthermore, local journalists are seen as "more caring, trustworthy, and neutral or unbiased."[41] Despite this perception, while struggling to survive and compete with national outlets, local media have also embraced "coverage of national partisan conflict" to satiate news consumers' diets.[42] As such, an interesting divergence of attitudes exists between Texans who primarily rely on local news and Texans who consume more national coverage. This is especially true when voters were asked to assess the performance of prominent elected officials.

Approval ratings for the two most prominent Republican candidates on the 2018 and 2020 ballots, respectively, find the unique roles both national and local selective media diets can play on individual attitudes. In short, viewers (and readers) of national news sources were less approving of both President Donald Trump and Texas Governor Greg Abbott, regardless of party affiliation. Overall, respondents who primarily use national media sources were overwhelmingly disapproving (55%) of Trump. Local media consumers were more approving (45%) than disapproving (41%). Abbott's approval was higher among local (64%) and national (52%) media users, but clearly weaker for the latter group.

This trend is clear among both parties. Thirty-one percent of Democrats who primarily watched local television news and read local newspapers (like the *Dallas Morning News* or the *Austin-American Statesman*) approved of Trump, compared with only 23 percent of Democrats whose main news sources were national network broadcasts (CBS, ABC, NBC, PBS), national cable news networks (CNN, Fox News, MSNBC), or national newspapers (*New York Times* or *Washington Post*). Governor Abbott's approval among Democrats who primarily watch local news was around 52 percent. This number plummets twelve points among Democrats who prefer national news outlets. A similar tendency exists among Republicans who get their news from local affiliates; they approved of Trump at 66 percent, eight points higher than Republicans who receive information from national outlets. Abbott's approval plummets ten points among Republicans when the coverage shifts from local to national news (80% to 70%).

This sort of local versus national coverage dynamic is also revealed on the question of the 2020 presidential vote choice. Overall, national media consumers were more likely to choose Joe Biden for president (54%) than Donald Trump (31%). But local media folks preferred the incumbent (45%) to the challenger (35%). "National Democrats" were more supportive of Democratic nominee Joe Biden (81%) than "local Democrats" (68%). Seventy-seven percent of "local Republicans" chose Donald Trump for president, while only 66 percent of "national Republicans" preferred the incumbent.

Yes, there is a partisan skew toward Democrats among all national media consumers. About 42 percent of national media consumers is made up of Democrats, compared with 36 percent of Republicans (and 22% of Independents). The same imbalance exists at the local media level. There are more Republican local media devotees (41%) than Democrats (33%). Nevertheless, the fact that we see nearly identical patterns within the parties suggests a significant local versus national media influence on voter attitudes and preferences.

One explanation for the discrepancy among Republicans is the significant differences between type of media coverage and age cohort. Republicans who are forty-five years and older were more likely than younger Republicans (ages eighteen to forty-four) to rely on local media for information. Meanwhile, younger Republicans were significantly more likely to use national media sources. We did not find a similar situation among Democrats, who—across all age groups—preferred national media.

Another factor to consider in the local and national coverage conversation is voter location. Texans living in rural communities are the one group overwhelmingly reliant upon national media coverage. Those living in larger population centers, from 250,000 to more than a million are to varying degrees more likely to consume local media. These residents live in communities that do not have strong local journalism, which creates an accessibility issue. In recent years, thousands of local newspapers have disappeared.[43] As such, "over sixty-five million Americans live in counties with only one local newspaper—or none at all."[44] Many of these "news deserts" are in "economically challenged rural places."[45] Since 2004, "146 weekly newspapers and 14 dailies have closed—half of them in rural areas."[46] The consequence of these closures—according to Darr, Hitt, and Dunaway—is that "readers consume more national news, which exposes people to intense political messages and increases polarized voting."[47] We find similar results, showing Texans who live in rural communities are significantly more likely than other community groups to identify as either "extremely liberal" or "extremely conservative," and are least likely to call themselves "moderate."

But local and national coverage is also competing with the ever-growing presence of social media—a medium tailor made for the sort of well-curated, selective, pro-attitudinal information bubble craved by media consumers.

Social Media and Selective Media Consumption

On January 8, 2021, President Donald Trump was permanently suspended from Twitter. That day, the social media Goliath released a public statement that cited two of Trump's tweets as "highly likely to encourage and inspire people to replicate the criminal acts that took place at the U.S. Capitol on January 6, 2021."[48] He was officially suspended for violating Twitter's "glorification of violence" policy. And with this act, the platform's most conspicuous political voice was gagged. Other platforms soon followed. By mid-January, Trump (and some of his most vocal allies) was banned by Facebook (now Meta), Instagram, YouTube, Snapchat, and Reddit. Meta's chief executive Mark Zuckerberg explained, "We believe the risks of allowing the President to continue to use our service during this period are simply too great."[49]

Prior to banning Trump in early 2021, conservatives had already expressed skepticism toward big tech giants like Google. A Pew Research survey in June 2020 found that 90 percent of Republicans say that social media sites censor political views.[50] Deplatforming the president was just more grist for the mill. Something—many conservatives believed—needed to be done about these powerful social media platforms. The solution—many argued—was for conservative social media users to move from "mainstream platforms such as Facebook and Twitter to less censored platforms such as Parler and Gab."[51]

As we continued to survey how Texans got their news in 2021, we found that the declining use of social media to find news was occurring at different rates by party. We found a 2 percent drop in the percentage of Democrats who primarily got their news from Facebook from 2020 to 2021, but no change with respect to the use of Twitter. Three percent fewer Republicans would acknowledge they got their news from Facebook in 2021. Still, the greatest decrease in the perceived value of social media as a news source was with Independents who saw a 5 percent decrease in the reliance on Facebook for news.

For their part, Democrats were less willing to buy the conservative line on this issue. That same Pew Research poll found about 59 percent of Democrats agreeing that censorship is happening on social media—a sure majority, but far less than among conservatives. Progressives have their own evidence to suggest that bias on social media is a figment of Republicans' imagination. For instance, they cite Facebook's daily top-most engaged link posts in the United States, which according to analysis by *New York Times* journalist Kevin Roose, is regularly dominated by conservative firebrands like Ben Shapiro and Dan Bongino. In fact, according to *POLITICO*, "Ben Shapiro, founding editor in chief of *The Daily Wire*, has logged over 175 million engagements on his Facebook page since June 21 [2020] compared with just 27 million for the *New York Times*' Facebook page."[52] Democratic skepticism is also supported by a recent report published by Barrett and Sims, which concludes that the GOP "bias-claim cudgel" is "based on distortions and falsehoods."[53]

In Texas, Republican politicians are doubling down on the bias claim. State Senator Bryan Hughes, an East Texas Republican, authored and proposed the "Protect Free Speech on Social Media" Act for the 2021 legislative session. This bill—supported by both Governor Greg Abbott and Lieutenant Governor Dan Patrick—would allow blocked or restricted social media users to sue to get back on the platforms and to recoup attorney's fees.[54]

In 2020 and 2021, we asked Texas voters from which social media platform they primarily obtain their news? With an understanding that the Trump ban was potentially a watershed moment in terms of partisan use of certain platforms, we wondered whether we would see any changes in Republican social media preferences in that time. We were also curious about Texans' overall social media preferences, what factors might alter these preferences (like age cohort), and whether a correlation exists between cable news preference and social media choice.

Overall, a plurality of Texans using social media were getting their news from Facebook. Around 42 percent of social media users chose Zuckerberg's conglomerate. Rounding out the top four platforms was Twitter (12%), YouTube (10%), and Other (22%).

We found that Republicans were more likely to cite Facebook (46%) than Democrats (39%), but the opposite was true for Twitter. That said, we did not find a significant correlation between platform use and partisan identification. Nonetheless, we discovered a small relationship between ideology and social media preference. Here, extreme liberals were most likely to use Tik Tok (23%), Instagram (20%), and Twitter (16%). Whereas extreme conservatives prefer Facebook (12%), WhatsApp (12%), Reddit (10%), or an unnamed Other (16%).

On the Left in particular, the age-related reputations of these platforms are important to acknowledge. As we have mentioned throughout the book, young people (ages sixteen to thirty-four) are more likely to identify as extremely liberal. And according to Tik Tok, they also happen to include about 80 percent of its users.[55] Instagram has a similar profile—where twenty-five- to thirty-four-year olds are the largest advertising audience.[56] When we looked at age cohorts, the least likely to use Facebook were eighteen to twenty-four-year olds (27%), who were also the most likely to cite Twitter (23%). Ages thirty-five to forty-four were the heaviest Facebook users (55%), while senior citizens were unsurprisingly the least likely group to use Twitter (3%). Among Texans, age cohort and social media platform choice are closely tied.

It is hard for us to argue that Republican Texans moved away from Twitter or Facebook for conservative alternatives in 2021. We do find Facebook and YouTube's share of the GOP social media preference increased from 2020 to 2021, while Twitter decreased, but we stop short of drawing firm conclusions. Our reticence is predicated on our comparably small sample size of Republican (and Democratic) social media users in our 2021 surveys. That said, there is some evidence that a GOP mass exodus from mainstream platforms is not likely to occur, even as alternatives appear. Barrett and Sims write, "Most conservatives aren't likely to retreat exclusively to their own corner of the social media world and cease paying attention to Facebook, Twitter, and YouTube. Conservatives are drawn to the established platforms for the same reason liberals are: That's where you can reach the largest audiences and enjoy the benefits of the network effect."[57]

Their assertion is further supported by polling data. A March 2021, The Hill/HarrisX survey found that only about 54 percent of Republicans intend to use a Trump-owned social media platform. It is unlikely that Republican social media habits will be drastically altered in the post-Trump ban era.

Discussion and Conclusion

If present selective media exposure is characterized by tuning in or turning off certain network television shows that feature popular political elites, an emerging frontier is social media. Much like Donald Trump—who revolutionized the platform as a means toward building a devoted political following and galvanizing free media coverage—officials are discovering ways to draw attention to (and humanize) themselves, bolster their relatability, and drive personal stories. For example, Texas congressman Dan Crenshaw is a prominent recent example of an elected official using platforms like Twitter to become a quasi-influencer, picking public fights with former-congressman Beto O'Rourke, castigating businesses for publicly denouncing Republican legislative initiatives, and sharing personal details about injuries sustained during a deployment in Afghanistan when he was wounded by an improvised explosive device (IED). And speaking of O'Rourke, during a winter storm crisis in 2021 in which millions of Texans lost power and water, the El Paso politician used social media to mobilize throngs of Americans to not only donate but also coordinate relief efforts. His tweets (and posts) garnered statewide attention, including speculation that he might be a viable challenger to Greg Abbott in the 2022 gubernatorial election.

Elite pivoting toward social media is also a financial necessity. Running for office in Texas—especially statewide—is an expensive endeavor because of the state's multiple media markets. Texas has six of Nielsen's Top 100 designated media markets in the United States—with Dallas/Fort Worth at fifth and Houston at eighth.[58] Consequently, political consultant Harold Cook guestimates that $20 million dollars is just barely enough to run a credible (but not necessarily winning) statewide race in Texas.[59] Most politicians are not going to raise that amount of money in any traditional sense, which is why social media, with its increasingly fertile fundraising capabilities, is where we expect more political elites to spend their time.

Two key questions about media habits in the post-COVID-19 era leave us plenty intrigued. First, are Texas Republicans going to become fragmented as their media choices expand? As noted, Fox News is currently dominating conservative attention on cable news, but will creeping competition from Newsmax TV and One America News Network (OANN)—both of which promise *fiercer* hyperpartisan coverage—splinter its audience share among Republicans? Will Texas Democratic habits parallel their national Democratic brethren? That is, are Texas Democrats going to become more hyperpartisan in media consumption (as suggested by national Democratic behavior) or will the moderate, cross-cutting sensibilities of the Biden era imbue their behavior?

CHAPTER 9

Texas's New Two-Party Dance

As the nation waits to see when or if Texas enters a new era of partisanship, residents are behaving as if they expect closer competition in the state elections. The rise of Republicans in Texas occurred over multiple elections, as Democrats and Independents crossed over to vote for a Republican for president. After fourteen years of challenging the solid Democratic Texas, Republicans took control of executive positions in Austin. The party had to keep fighting nine more years to gain control of the state legislature. The fissures which have weakened the foundation of the Texas-sized Republican advantage are still young and lack an established leader who can help voters crossover to prefer another party to lead the state. Concurrently, Republicans are mitigating some urban losses by recruiting candidates in areas of the Rio Grande Valley where Democrats previously saw little opposition. As a result, both parties have worked to try to give voters a reason to participate in the state elections.

Our polling of Texans during this time of exceptional political change calls into question whether past conclusions from scholars of public opinion and Southern politics still apply to Texas. The first assumption that should be revisited is that race is less important in Texas politics than other Southern states. In this book we have analyzed what characteristics shape who joins a party coalition and examined the dynamics of rhetoric used to mobilize voters only to find that race matters more than economic status as a determinant of political views at this time. Second, we did not find that Texas voters are becoming more conservative. Perhaps the closeness of statewide elections or changing demographics are strong enough associations that this point is already in question. We have discussed how the context of the elections have mattered from our finding that more voters were likely to feel they were moderate in 2018 than 2020. Also, we are seeing the margin of victory for Republicans in the counties that surround the urban centers is declining.

V. O. Key expressed doubt that race mattered in Texas's politics.[1] That perspective was expressed before immigration quotas were lifted and the Latino population in Texas began to rise. Still, many scholars have continued this assumption because of low rates of voter turnout among Latino voters in the state. Moreover, there was ideological diversity within the Latino electorate that precluded either party from gaining a sustained advantage by attracting the block of voters to their coalition.

Race is becoming a powerful factor within Texas's party primary politics. On the Democratic side, the absence from winning statewide elections has made the effect of race vary from election to election. In 2018, U.S. Representative Beto O'Rourke avoided most issues of race within the Democratic Party because the party prioritized viability to give a strong challenge to Senator Ted Cruz. In the 2018 Democratic primary, lesser-known activist Sema Hernandez captured 24 percent of the votes and raised the question of whether O'Rourke would have a problem with Latino voters. In 2020, none of the sitting members of Congress emerged to run against Senator John Cornyn, so race became one of the defining characteristics of each candidate. This Democratic primary became divisive over race as it moved to a run-off. The third-place candidate, Christina Tzintzún Ramirez, endorsed State Senator Royce West to mobilize Black and Latino support behind one nominee. That action was unsuccessful, but a point of concern to unify the Texas Democratic Party in the general election was that MJ Hegar and State Senator West did not heal the wounds after the run-off. Senator West stated publicly that he would not vote for her and, "she's had a problem all along with black folks."[2] The absence of coordination between past rivals does not necessarily mean there are clear racial divisions in the Democratic Party, but it does ascribe a complication with the candidate-centered nature of a party without a clear standard bearer.

The notion that the Democratic Party cannot win Texas with a cohesive block of Black voters and some White voters is still true. Black voters only make up 14 percent of the registered voters in Texas, which makes the issues somewhat more complex when we consider how Blacks in the electorate are likely to agree with Latino and a portion of White voters. The reason the issue of race as a motivator in which candidate voters choose is notable to this time period is that Whites make up less than 57 percent of all registered voters, even though estimates suggest 60 percent of all voters in 2018 and 2020 were White. Also, Huerta and Cuartas found that the balance of White voters more supportive of the Republican party is positively associated with age, even though the age difference is less likely to be found among other race and ethnicities.[3] Previously, the majority party in Texas could succeed despite ideological diversity within the White electorate. Today that margin of diversity is a liability in safely winning elections. The context becomes even more concerning because Texas Democrats do not appear to defect from their strategy in the past twenty-four years to elevate the discussion of race in the state as a younger Latino population ascends to an eligible voting age.

Enns and Koch suggest Texas's ideology in the 2000s was moderately conservative and is becoming more conservative.[4] In chapter one, we point out this observation was made at a time when the Texas Democratic Party resigned itself to a regional and urban party in the state. Voter turnout was low, which is emblematic of lower voter engagement across the state. Individuals who are less interested in politics are also less likely to take surveys.

We have been fortunate to conduct surveys during a time when political interest across Texas is high and people want to share their opinions. The increased belief that each vote in Texas matters more today allows us to confirm that Texas's ideology is indeed moderately conservative, but we would challenge the notion that it is on a trend to become more conservative. We find the growing Latino electorate is also moderate in their ideology, even as they opt out of voting for the more conservative and populist candidates in the state's elections. The center-right status of the electorate means they are not as loyal to the Democratic Party as Black voters but do support Democratic candidates more than White voters.

In presidential elections, placing Texas as a "toss-up" has implications for any candidate's Electoral College strategy. After the 2020 Census, Texas gained two more seats in the U.S. House, which increased the number of Texas's electors in the Electoral College to forty. Texas also has the largest number of delegates to award to a presidential candidate among the 164 electors who can be won from the eleven states in the South.

Future candidates and party leaders would be wise to consider what policy topics they should discuss when looking for a way to wedge voters from their current party identification. Our experience polling voters in the past few years has shown that policy debates that center around law enforcement often harden a voter's commitment to their party. If Republicans success-fully frame the issue in terms of safety, they have an opportunity to maintain support among a more traditionalistic coalition. When issues related to law enforcement are tied to race, Democratic candidates have found ways to mo-bilize greater turnout among voters. As a result, race is emerging as an issue that is framing the future of Texas politics in ways that balance safety, oppor-tunity, and fairness.

We have also seen two elections where candidates at the top of the ticket have engaged in contentious debates about the wall along the U.S.-Mexico border. Few Texans lack an opinion on the topic, but it is old enough that it is no longer a wedge to cross-pressure voters in either direction based on the attention it occupies. Studying public attitudes on this question alongside others bears out the possibility that beliefs about the border wall are largely shaped by what party a voter aligns themselves with. This is because party identification presents the clearest difference in attitudes, whereas race and ethnicity did not. Part of the explanation lies within the context of the issue. Residents of El Paso and the Rio Grande Valley already live in a community where a border wall exists. Much of the debate on this topic is chatter away from the border deciding whether more barriers are needed in the least pop-ulated areas. These latter points help us understand why we would be incor-rect to assume that the border wall is a hot button issue. Talking about the border wall does not alienate enough voters in the communities that do not have a barrier in their community as much as it energizes people in more dis-tant communities.[5]

The issues that consistently attract the attention of voters are tied to the culture war and economics. Republican candidates are reaching out to voters on a different dimension. Most often the frame from state leaders also limits the ability of Democratic candidates to pivot to a more popular position. In this case, public disagreement about a pathway to citizenship typically dis-tracts leaders from debating their common support for deferred action for childhood arrivals (DACA). Party and ideology drive most of our politics. Race matters on certain issues, the nomination process, and a voter's willing-ness to self-identify with a party. The parties are less competitive, because there are fewer White voters who associate with the Democratic Party in Texas than other Southern states.

The voting choices of the Latino electorate is important for the future, because they affiliate with the Democratic party less than other non-White constituencies. While the Latino electorate is not homogenous, there are more precise identities that have similar views including the Tejanos who pre-date statehood, Mexican Americans whose grandparents were born in Texas, and newly naturalized citizens from Central America. Still, these are the vot-ers who make Texas a triethnic state. The U.S. Census estimates that three ethnic/racial groups contribute more than 10 percent of the population of Texas: White (41%); Hispanic (40%); and African American (12%). These demographics suggest that anyone who would win Texas in the primary or the general election must appeal to more than one ethnic or racial group to be successful.

For decades, Texas Republicans have been appealing to many Latinos by emphasizing economic issues and taking a different tact than national Re-publicans, since the comprehensive immigration plan supported by President George W. Bush failed in 2007. Texas Republicans continued to follow the approach of Governor Bush, while national Republicans became more hard-line on the issue. Texas Republicans have rarely been antagonistic toward the Latino population or applied stereotypes. When elected officials have made derogatory comments, lawmakers have been careful to target those comments to people who are not from Texas. Even then, the harshest rhetoric is often not followed by government action.

Texas Republicans also appear to be making efforts to retain support from other constituencies who were less enthusiastic about the party nationally, including White women. This has been done by encouraging women to hold leadership positions. Representative Beth Van Duyne became the second fe-male Republican to be elected to the U.S. House from Texas, twenty-four years after Representative Kay Granger (R-TX) won her first election. Then in a follow up to the 2020 election, Susan Wright was recruited to run in a 2021 special election to succeed her husband who died shortly after the No-vember election. The party has also intentionally highlighted the influence of Vice Chairwoman Cat Parks, the second highest-ranking person in the Texas GOP.

The strategy to recruit female candidates under the Republican ticket and emphasize issues within the frame of safety has led to a steady increase in the party identification of White women. In 2018, 53 percent of the White women we surveyed either identified or leaned to the Republican Party. The affinity for the GOP within this voting block increased each year, by 1 percent in 2019, then to 56 percent in 2020, and 60 percent in early 2021. The positive trend overstates the support the party has among all women. A comparison of the party identification of female voters in 2018 and 2021 shows that the larger demographic has not changed at all (46% Democratic, 41% Republican). The rise of White women within the Republican Party is masking the declining connection the Republican Party has among Latinas across the state.

Our pooled set of all surveys shows a clear drop in the partisan identification of Latinas in the Republican Party. In 2018, we first found 35 percent of Latina voters identified with the Republican Party. In 2019, on average only 21 percent of Latina voters felt that they were Republicans. We cannot pin point the cause of this shift, but President Trump threatened ICE raids in the South on multiple occasions, family separations continued, and at a more local level families in the Borderlands like Webb County received notices that the federal government had requested access to their property to survey land for construction of the border wall.[6] Amid all of the possible explanations, this was the period of time when Latina voters disapproved of Donald Trump the most. During the last two years of his term, Latina voters admonished the President's job 9 percent more often than Latino voters (23% approve, 63% disapprove). Efforts to mobilize ahead of the election brought the party identification of Latina Republicans back up to 26 percent in 2020. Now that Trump has left office, more Latina voters are willing to identify with the Republican Party again (30% Republican, 18% Neither).

The whole picture painted by these interesting puzzle pieces is that Texas voters are unique and attracting their support takes special skill, responsiveness to diverse communities and regions, and an ability to differentiate Texas from the rest of the nation. For the reasons we have just listed, Texas's political culture is most clearly tied to the relative difference between the nominees at any given time. These voters who in the past have rewarded name recognition and swagger are taking more time to decide whom they will support when there is not an incumbent's record to compare. We saw this with the large number of voters on Super Tuesday who waited to decide who they would support in the 2020 Democratic primary for president.

After Texas supported Donald Trump in 2016 and 2020, voters have shown greater interest in candidates from outside the party establishment. Texas, as represented by Ted Cruz and Dan Patrick, contrasts with its preexisting advantage for candidates who rise within their party establishment. What is also clear is that a candidate does not need to be a party warrior. Candidates like Beto O'Rourke were able to develop similar grassroots support as Bernie Sanders by being the candidate voters trust to tell it like it is. When Matthew McConaughey flirted with the idea of running to be governor of Texas, the public used the same frame to evaluate the idea. McConaughey's "honesty, to tell it like it is," was the primary characteristic that attracted his potential supporters. These candidates get an initial spark, but the grit and determination of Republicans who prove to be empathetic to the entire state are more difficult to beat because of they appeal to the voters who are slightly conservative on both sides of the aisle.

Texas has become a toss-up, but that means its political future will be defined over a gradual period and not in a single election, just like it has been before. We are in a moment where those with moderate to conservative views are a large enough electorate to determine who may receive the second largest count of Electoral College votes in a presidential election. This is the dilemma for the Democratic National Committee. The largest cities in Texas are major sources of campaign contributions for candidates at the national stage, including progressive candidates. The largest cities are also where most of the Democrats elected to federal office serve. Winning in new areas across the state and regaining the legacy of Lyndon B. Johnson requires effort and more communities. Beto O'Rourke exposed the relative advantage for Republicans hold in the towns with less than 250,000 residents and how so much of that is developed by showing up. No doubt, these are some of the most conservative areas of the state, and as we discussed they vote 2 to 1 for Republicans. That relative advantage exists as Democrats vote share underperform the estimates of party identification we found in these communities.

Down ballot races in 2018 and 2020 showed that Texas Republicans have had to expend more resources to protect the depth of their power in the state. In 2018, Texas Democrats defeated nineteen incumbent judges on the Texas Court of Appeals and succeeded in flipping partisan control of four of the fourteen districts. The Democrats issued another challenge in 2020 to try to defeat incumbent Republicans in the Texas House who served in urban and suburban districts. Despite help by the party and Powered by the People, the Democratic candidate narrowly lost in seventeen key races that could have split the partisan control of the Texas Legislature. Moreover, the turnover in partisan judicial elections in 2018 motivated Governor Greg Abbott to dedicate his time to campaigning to elect Republican judges down the ballot. The small proxy wars between Texas Republicans and Texas Democrats in the last year have been fascinating, but they are also a preview of how the parties will develop the next generation of leaders and try to connect with voters in regions across the state.

APPENDIX

Table A.1: Likelihood of Partisan Strength among Texas Voters, Relative to Selecting Strong Republican

Variable	Choice	All	SE	2018	SE	2019	SE	2020	SE	2021	SE
White	Strong Dem	-0.31	0.28	-1.99*	0.53	-0.24	0.72	-0.66*	0.26	0.07	0.28
	Weak Dem	-0.78*	0.24	-1.97*	0.52	-0.35	0.53	-1.04*	0.25	-0.80*	0.27
	Moderate	-0.67*	0.26	-0.28	0.55	0.31	0.73	-1.13*	0.26	-0.81*	0.30
	Weak Rep.	-0.27	0.22	-0.98	0.59	-0.03	0.62	-0.58*	0.25	-0.09	0.29
Latino	Strong Dem	1.06*	0.30	-0.94	0.64	1.43	0.76	1.44*	0.32	0.95*	0.32
	Weak Dem	0.59*	0.27	-0.83	0.66	0.80	0.64	0.96*	0.32	0.49	0.30
	Moderate	0.48	0.29	-0.51	0.68	1.56	0.83	0.48	0.33	0.30	0.33
	Weak Rep.	0.38	0.26	-0.44	0.72	0.43	0.75	0.46	0.33	0.39	0.35
Black	Strong Dem	2.20*	0.33	1.55	0.82	2.14*	0.82	2.60*	0.41	2.05*	0.38
	Weak Dem	1.15*	0.32	0.45	0.86	1.66*	0.73	1.33*	0.40	0.98*	0.37
	Moderate	0.66	0.34	0.81	0.83	0.47	1.09	0.73	0.42	0.57	0.41
	Weak Rep.	0.13	0.33	-0.41	1.05	-0.72	0.88	-0.10	0.55	0.43	0.42
Female	Strong Dem	0.22*	0.08	0.33	0.22	0.52*	0.23	0.14	0.10	0.09	0.11
	Weak Dem	0.19*	0.08	0.27	0.23	0.44	0.24	0.01	0.11	0.13	0.12
	Moderate	0.17*	0.09	0.30	0.25	0.30	0.39	0.12	0.13	0.03	0.13
	Weak Rep.	-0.14	0.13	0.61*	0.24	-0.65*	0.32	-0.08	0.17	-0.13	0.19
25–34	Strong Dem	-0.14	0.24	-1.23	0.64	-0.94	0.49	0.39	0.32	0.84*	0.35
	Weak Dem	-0.38	0.27	-1.34*	0.61	-1.49*	0.52	0.28	0.32	0.25	0.35
	Moderate	-0.31	0.27	-1.50*	0.60	-0.02	0.62	0.05	0.37	-0.16	0.42
	Weak Rep.	-0.51	0.26	-1.10	0.68	-1.39*	0.50	-0.14	0.37	0.42	0.42
35–44	Strong Dem	0.38	0.23	-0.36	0.65	-0.20	0.45	0.70*	0.32	1.09*	0.34
	Weak Dem	-0.13	0.26	-1.11	0.63	-0.93*	0.47	0.39	0.31	0.24	0.34
	Moderate	0.17	0.26	-0.91	0.60	0.28	0.62	0.59	0.34	0.13	0.41
	Weak Rep.	-0.37	0.25	-0.66	0.68	-0.98*	0.46	0.26	0.36	-0.01	0.42
45–64	Strong Dem	0.08	0.22	0.68	0.68	-0.25	0.60	1.06*	0.30	0.78*	0.32
	Weak Dem	-0.25	0.25	-0.03	0.66	-0.97	0.64	0.72*	0.30	0.16	0.32
	Moderate	0.41	0.25	-0.53	0.65	0.07	0.76	0.98*	0.33	0.51	0.40
	Weak Rep.	-0.19	0.24	-0.66	0.74	-0.38	0.59	0.39	0.36	-0.01	0.37
65+	Strong Dem	0.22	0.23	0.48	0.63	-0.58	0.46	1.25*	0.30	0.81*	0.33

		b	SE	b	SE	b	SE	b	SE	b	SE
	Weak Dem	-0.42	0.27	-0.81	0.60	-1.27*	0.52	0.60*	0.29	0.12	0.34
	Moderate	-0.15	0.25	-0.93	0.59	-0.63	0.56	0.66*	0.33	0.17	0.43
	Weak Rep.	-0.41	0.24	-1.03	0.68	-0.86*	0.44	0.16	0.36	-0.10	0.37
Bachelors	Strong Dem	0.35*	0.10	0.35	0.27	0.23	0.25	0.17	0.14	0.69*	0.16
	Weak Dem	0.32*	0.10	0.40	0.30	0.51*	0.25	0.10	0.14	0.50*	0.16
	Moderate	0.01	0.11	0.01	0.28	0.36	0.33	-0.01	0.16	0.00	0.19
	Weak Rep.	0.23*	0.11	0.50	0.37	0.07	0.26	0.30*	0.15	0.24	0.18
Income	Strong Dem	-0.09*	0.03	-0.16*	0.06	-0.14*	0.05	-0.08*	0.03	-0.08	0.04
	Weak Dem	-0.13*	0.03	-0.22*	0.08	-0.21*	0.06	-0.05	0.03	-0.14*	0.05
	Moderate	-0.09*	0.03	-0.10	0.06	0.01	0.09	-0.02	0.04	-0.15*	0.06
	Weak Rep.	0.01	0.03	-0.16*	0.07	0.05	0.06	0.04	0.03	0.01	0.05
Evangelical	Strong Dem	-0.11	0.12	-1.53*	0.38	1.17*	0.32	-0.90*	0.20	-0.65*	0.21
	Weak Dem	-0.79*	0.14	-1.57*	0.39	-0.27	0.40	-1.27*	0.20	-1.08*	0.24
	Moderate	-0.57*	0.15	-0.63	0.36	-0.21	0.49	-0.83*	0.23	-1.04*	0.27
	Weak Rep.	-0.26	0.14	-1.23*	0.46	1.00*	0.36	-0.31	0.20	-0.60*	0.21
Catholic	Strong Dem	0.14	0.13	-0.30	0.43	0.60	0.37	-0.48*	0.20	-0.21	0.19
	Weak Dem	-0.06	0.16	-0.22	0.44	0.42	0.42	-0.63*	0.20	-0.21	0.21
	Moderate	-0.61*	0.16	-0.39	0.46	-0.46	0.47	-0.69*	0.22	-0.88*	0.24
	Weak Rep.	-0.72*	0.16	-0.91	0.55	-0.70	0.43	-0.75*	0.23	-0.76*	0.26
Mainline	Strong Dem	0.22	0.16	-1.54*	0.47	0.97*	0.44	-0.36	0.19	-0.05	0.21
	Weak Dem	0.30	0.19	-0.96	0.58	1.41*	0.45	-0.36	0.19	-0.30	0.22
	Moderate	-0.20	0.16	-1.11*	0.48	0.67	0.47	-0.49*	0.23	-0.65*	0.26
	Weak Rep.	-0.17	0.15	-1.17*	0.58	0.58	0.43	-0.25	0.22	-0.25	0.25
Conservative	Strong Dem	-2.58*	0.10	-3.09*	0.33	-0.67*	0.26	-3.81*	0.17	-3.23*	0.16
	Weak Dem	-2.61*	0.15	-3.02*	0.35	-0.71*	0.32	-3.54*	0.18	-3.44*	0.19
	Moderate	-2.73*	0.14	-2.36*	0.32	-2.05*	0.55	-3.11*	0.20	-3.22*	0.24
	Weak Rep.	-0.79*	0.12	0.89	0.57	-1.12*	0.29	-0.78*	0.18	-0.91*	0.18
Cons	Strong Dem	0.63	0.35	4.09	0.85	-0.09	0.82	0.97	0.38	0.02	0.40
	Weak Dem	1.75	0.33	4.68	0.85	1.04	0.68	1.71	0.37	1.86	0.36
	Moderate	1.13	0.34	2.68	0.84	-1.19	0.92	0.93	0.39	2.06	0.41
	Weak Rep.	0.09	0.33	0.04	1.07	-0.07	0.72	-0.55	0.41	0.13	0.50
N =		9.95		897		1,745		3,514		3.39	
F =		30.89		4.53		17.82		16.98			

Table A.2: Likelihood of Supporting Republican Candidate in Texas

Variable	Abbott	SE	Cruz	SE	Cornyn	SE	Trump	SE
Constant	-4.76*	0.80	-7.67*	1.05	-7.58*	1.44	-9.87*	1.54
Party ID (5 point scale)	1.08*	0.11	1.30*	0.12	1.56*	0.16	2.13**	0.21
Ideology	0.42*	0.08	0.42*	0.08	0.60*	0.14	0.63*	0.14
White	-0.12	0.49	1.37*	0.57	0.12	0.62	0.71	0.68
Latino	-0.99*	0.55	0.47	0.65	0.04	0.78	-0.83	0.88
Black	-1.24*	0.71	-0.51	0.83	0.06	0.97	-0.92	1.18
Catholic	0.03	0.55	0.11	0.64	-0.34	0.73	-1.15	0.77
Evangelical	0.23	0.56	0.04	0.63	0.06	0.78	-0.29	0.80
Mainline Protestant	-0.33	0.59	-0.59	0.67	-0.02	0.72	-1.41*	0.74
Black Protestant	0.94	0.89	0.82	1.15	0.05	1.39	-1.79	1.34
Secular	-0.12	0.57	0.21	0.64	0.43	2.56	-0.03	3.24
Attend Worship	-0.08	0.11	-0.11	0.11	0.16	0.18	0.12	0.19
Importance of Religion	0.43*	0.16	0.56*	0.17	0.04	0.19	0.13	0.20
Age	-0.12	0.10	-0.13	0.11	0.61*	0.36	0.52	0.38
Gender	0.48*	0.25	0.75*	0.28	-0.05	0.15	-0.31*	0.17
Married			-0.07	0.11	0.22	0.39	0.68*	0.39
Income			-0.03	0.13	-0.16	0.13		
N =	754		721		564		661	
Cox and Snell R^2	0.50		0.56		0.59		0.65	

NOTES

Foreword

1. Autullo, Ryan and Nicole Cobler, "Did Austin police cuts play role in Texas Democrats' election woes?" *Austin American-Statesman*, November 6, 2020. Website: https://www.statesman.com/story/news/politics/elections/2020/11/06/did-austin-police-cuts-play-role-in-texas-democratsrsquo-election-woes/114721392/

2. Adams.

3. Garrett, Robert T., "Abbott has 'Ideas' on Protecting Police Funding," *Dallas Morning News*, 9B, January 15, 2021.

4. Phillips, Kevin. *The Emerging Republican Majority* (Princeton: Princeton University Press, 1969), 13-17.

5. Garrett, Robert T. and Lauren McGaughy, "Income Tax Idea Headed to Voters," *Dallas Morning News*, 9B, May 22, 2019.

6. D'Annunzio, Francesca. 2022. "GOP rivals spar for new Collin seat in House." *Dallas Morning News*, 7A. February 27, 2022.

7. Judis, John B. and Ruy Teixeira, *The Emerging Democratic Majority* (New York: Simon and Schuster, 2002), 34-35, 59, 61, 165, 177.

8. Potter, Lloyd, "Demograhic Trends and Projections in Texas," Presentation to Texas Associated Press Managers in San Angelo, TX, October 16, 2021, Slides 6, 50-51. Link: https://demographics.texas.gov/Resources/Presentations/OSD/2021/2021_10_16_TexasAssociatedPressManagingEditors.pdf

9. Jillson, Cal, *Lone Star Tarnished: A Critical Look at Texas Politics and Public Policy*, Second Edition (New York: Routledge, 2015), 4.

Chapter 1: Political Change in Texas

1. Jamie Lovegrove, "El Paso Democrat to challenge Ted Cruz," *Dallas Morning News* 3B, April 1, 2017; https://www.dallasnews.com/news/politics/2017/03/31/beto-o-rourke-launches-2018-senate-campaign-in-underdog-bid-to-unseat-ted-cruz/.

2. John Gerring, *Party Ideologies in America, 1828–1996* (Cambridge: Cambridge University Press, 2001).

3. Valdimer Orlando Key, *Southern Politics in State and Nation*, vol. 510 (New York: Knopf, 1949). Robert S. Erikson, Gerald C. Wright, and John P. McIver, *Statehouse Democracy: Public Opinion and Policy in the American States* (New York: Cambridge University Press, 1993).

4. Earl Black and Merle Black, *The Rise of Southern Republicans* (Cambridge, MA: Harvard University Press, 2002), 88–91.

5. Ibid., 268–93

6. Joel Silbey, *Storm over Texas: The Annexation Controversy and the Road to Civil War* (Oxford: Oxford University Press, 2007).

7. Texas Secretary of State website, "Presidential Election Results." Accessed April 26, 2021; https://www.sos.state.tx.us/elections/historical/index.shtml.

8. Bryan Burrough, *The Big Rich: The Rise and Fall of the Greatest Texas Oil Fortunes* (New York: Penguin, 2009).

9. David Lublin describes this as named for the soil, not the people, but the largely rural, agricultural areas of the Deep South that also have heavy Black populations; see *The Republican South*, Princeton University Press, 2004.

10. Sanford N. Greenberg, *The Handbook of Texas*, Texas State Historical Association, Published September 29, 2020; https://www.tshaonline.org/handbook /entries/white-primary.

11. Charles S. Bullock III and Ronald Keith Gaddie, *The Triumph of Voting Rights in the South* (Norman: University of Oklahoma Press, 2009).

12. Louisiana voted for Democratic nominee Adlai Stevenson in 1952, but not in 1956.

13. New York remained the most populous state with forty-three congressional districts (down two). California became tied with Pennsylvania as the second most populous state with thirty congressional districts by adding seven, while Pennsylvania lost three. Illinois lost one seat and slid to become the fourth most populous state. Ohio remained the fifth most populous state with one more congressional district than Texas.

14. Alan S. Gerber, Gregory A. Huber, Conor M. Dowling, David Doherty, and Nicole Schwartzberg, "Using Battleground States as a Natural Experiment to Test Theories of Voting," Presented at the American Political Science Association meeting (Toronto), September 3–6, 2009; https://huber.research.yale.edu/materials /74_paper.pdf.

15. Neal Tannahill, *Texas Government: Policy and Politics*, 8th ed. (New York: Pearson, 2005).

16. After the all-White primary ended, Texas was the only Southern state that

did not have a mechanism to disenfranchise voters solely based on race. Texas counties levied poll taxes to cover the cost of elections, which suppressed turnout. The adoption of the Twenty Fourth Amendment in 1964 ended the practice of counties charging poll taxes in federal elections. Shortly thereafter, the U.S. Supreme Court ruled in *Harper v. Virginia State Board of Elections* (1966) a requirement that citizens pay to vote for state elections was a violation of the Fourteenth Amendment.

17. The other two criteria include whether the language minority population was more than 5 percent of the voting-age population and if more than 5 percent of the Indian American citizens live on a reservation. See Voting Rights Act Amendments of 2006, Determinations Under Section 203, Public Law 109–246, *U.S. Statutes at Large* 120(2006): 577–81.

18. M. V. Hood III and Seth C. McKee, "Texas: Big Red Rides On," in Charles S. Bullock III and Mark J. Rozell, eds., *The New Politics of the Old South: An Introduction to Southern Politics*, 6th ed. (Lanham, MD: Rowman & Littlefield, 2018).

19. Robert S. Erikson, Gerald C. Wright, and John P. McIver, *Statehouse Democracy: Public Opinion and Policy in the American States* (New York: Cambridge University Press, 1993).

20. Black and Black, *Rise of Southern Republicans*, 211–29. Marjorie Randon Hershey, *Party Politics in America*, 17th ed. (New York: Routledge, 2017).

21. Erikson, Wright, and McIver, *Statehouse Democracy*.

22. Black and Black, *Rise of Southern Republicans*, 23–24.

23. Bullock and Gaddie, *Triumph of Voting Rights in the South*.

24. Ibid.

25. Hood and McKee, "Texas: Big Red Rides On."

26. Ronald Brownstein, "Texas 'Dream Team' Carries Democrats' Hopes," *Los Angeles Times*, October 19, 2020; https://www.latimes.com/archives/la-xpm-2002 -oct-19-na-dream19-story.html.

27. The CNN ratings have been used in public opinion research to indicate how experts view the competitiveness of an election prior to Election Day. See https:// www.cnn.com/election/2020/electoral-college-interactive-maps#build-your-own. Costas Panagopoulos, "Campaign Dynamics in Battleground and Nonbattleground States," *Public Opinion Quarterly* 73, no. 1 (2009): 119–29.

28. Editorial Board, "We Recommend Hillary Clinton for President," *Dallas Morning News* 20A, September 7, 2016; https://www.dallasnews.com/opinion /editorials/2016/09/07/we-recommend-hillary-clinton-for-president/.

29. Characteristic of a traditionalistic state's institutions being designed to maintain the existing political and social order is Texas's tradition of holding partisan elections for all state judges, even at the appellate level, complete with financing these elections by plaintiff and defense lawyers. See Donald W. Jackson and James

W. Riddlesperger Jr., "Money and Politics in Judicial Elections: The 1988 Election of the Chief Justice of the Texas Supreme Court," *Judicature* 74 (December–January 1991): 184–89.

30. Daniel J. Elazar, *American Federalism: A View from the States*, 3rd ed. (New York: Harper and Row, 1984).

31. Chandler Davidson, *Race and Class in Texas Politics* (Princeton, NJ: Princeton University Press, 1990).

32. Hood and McKee, "Texas: Big Red Rides On"; Susan MacManus, "The Appropriateness of Biracial Approaches to Measuring Fairness of Representation in a Multicultural World," *PS: Political Science and Politics* 28 (March 1995): 42–47.

33. Seth C. McKee, Jeremy M. Teigen, and Mathieu Turgeon, "The Partisan Impact of Congressional Redistricting: The Case of Texas, 2001–2003," *Social Science Quarterly* 87 (2): 308–17; and John R. Petrocik and Scott W. Desposato, "The Partisan Consequences of Majority-Minority Redistricting in the South, 1992 and 1994," *Journal of Politics* 60 (3): 613–33.

34. Lublin, *The Republican South*, chapter 6.

35. U.S. Census Bureau, "Metropolitan and Micropolitan Statistical Areas Population Totals and Components of Change: 2010–2019."

36. Edward G. Carmines and James A. Stimson, "Issue Evolution, Population Replacement, and Normal Partisan Change," *American Political Science Review* 75 (March 1981): 107–18; Lublin, *The Republican South*, chapter 6.

Chapter 2: New Party Coalitions in Texas

1. Paul Burka, "George W. Bush and the New Political Landscape," *Texas Monthly*, December 1994.

2. Wayne Thorburn, *Red State: An Insider's Story of How the GOP Came to Dominate Texas Politics* (Austin: University of Texas Press, 2013).

3. John Petrocik, *Party Coalitions: Realignments and the Decline of the New Deal Party System* (Chicago: University of Chicago Press, 1981).

4. Alan A. Abramowitz, *The Great Alignment: Race, Party Transformation, and the Rise of Donald Trump* (New Haven, CT: Yale University Press, 2018); Paul R. Abramson, John H. Aldrich, and David W. Rohde, *Change and Continuity in the 2008 and 2010 Elections* (Washington, DC: CQ Press, 2012); Larry M. Bartels, "Partisanship and Voting Behavior, 1952–1996," *American Journal of Political Science* 44 (2000): 35–50; Paul Allen Beck, Lawrence Baum, Aage R. Clausen, and Charles E. Smith Jr., "Patterns and Sources of Ticket Splitting in Subpresidential Voting," *American Political Science Review* 86 (1992): 916–28; Angus Campbell,

Philip E. Converse, Warren E. Miller, and Donald E. Stokes, *The American Voter* (New York: John Wiley and Sons, 1960); James E. Campbell, *The American Campaign: U.S. Presidential Campaigns and Pre-National Vote* (College Station: Texas A&M University Press, 2000); Michael S. Lewis-Beck, William G. Jacoby, Helmut Norpoth, and Herbert F. Weisberg, *The American Voter Revisited* (Ann Arbor: University of Michigan Press, 2008).

5. We maintain that ideology comes first, followed by party identification, but that as one casts votes for the same party, party identification becomes the more important and stable of the two over time. It should also be noted that one's view of candidate characteristics (which candidate has the most relevant experience, the higher level of character and ethics, and so forth) can be affected by one's partisanship, as can one's appraisal of which candidate takes the "best" positions on the issues.

6. Lewis-Beck, et al., *American Voter Revisited*; D. Sunshine Hillygus and Todd G. Shields, *The Persuadable Voter: Wedge Issues in Presidential Campaigns* (Princeton, NJ: Princeton University Press, 2008).

7. In following convention, we asked survey respondents about their party identifications. Based on the three questions noted earlier, we were able to categorize each respondent who gave us answers to the questions, as 1–7. In our scheme, strong Democrats were coded 1, weak Democrats were coded 2, Independent "Leaners" toward the Democrats were coded 3, Pure Independents were coded 4, Independent "Leaners" toward the Republicans were coded 5, weak Republicans were coded 6, and strong Republicans were coded 7.

8. Gromer Jeffers, "GOP Outworked Dems in Texas," *Dallas Morning News* 1A, November 5, 2020;

9. Ibid.

10. In later analyses in this chapter and in later chapters, we will use a party identification variable coded as 1–5, with 1 representing strong Democrats, 2 representing weak Democrats and Democratic "leaners," 3 representing pure Independents, 4 representing weak Republicans and Republican "leaners," and 5 representing strong Republicans (the "5-point" scale).

11. David B. Magleby, Candice J. Nelson, and Mark C. Westlye, "The Myth of the Independent Voter Revisited," in Paul M. Sniderman and Benjamin Highton, eds., *Facing the Challenge of Democracy* (Princeton, NJ: Princeton University Press, 2011), 238–63.

12. Our five-level index for education (high school or less, some college, associate degree, bachelor's degree, or graduate degree) is correlated with party identification at .000 in 2018 and .041 in 2020.

13. Aldrich, John H., Jamie L. Carson, Brad T. Gomez, and David W. Rohde.,

Change and Continuity in the 2016 and 2018 Elections (Thousand Oaks, CA: CQ Press, 2020).

14. Petrocik, *Party Coalitions*; Jeffrey M. Stonecash, *Class and Party in American Politics* (Boulder, CO: Westview Press, 2000). The Pearson's r correlation between household income and party identification is .204 in 2018 (p < .01, two-tailed) and .101 in 2020 (p < .01, two-tailed).

15. Juan Carol Huerta and Beatriz Cuartas, "Red to Purple? Changing Demographics and Party Change in Texas," *Social Sciences Quarterly* 102, no. 4(2021): 1330-48.

16. Aldrich, et al., *Change and Continuity in the 2016 and 2018 Elections.*

17. Thornburn, *Red State*, p. 223.

18. Petrocik, *Party Coalitions*; Kenneth D. Wald, *Religion and Politics in the United States,* 3rd ed. (Washington, DC: Congressional Quarterly, 1997.)

19. Marjorie Randon Hershey, *Party Politics in America,* 17th ed. (New York: Routledge, 2017); David Lublin, *The Republican South: Democratization and Partisan Change* (Princeton, NJ: Princeton University Press, 2004).

20. Corwin E. Smidt, *American Evangelicals Today* (Lanham, MD: Rowman & Littlefield, 2013); Wald, *Religion and Politics in the United States.*

21. Abramowitz, *The Great Alignment*; Aldrich, et al., *Change and Continuity in the 2016 and 2018 Elections.*

22. Petrocik, *Party Coalitions*. Petrocik considered ethnoreligious variables (not just Protestants, Catholics, and Jews but "German Protestants," "Blacks," "Anglo-Saxon Protestants," and so forth), the region of the country where a respondent lived, "the size and place of residence" of the respondent, the education of the respondent, and the "occupational status" of the respondent.

23. Thornburn, *Red State.*

24. Alex Samuels, "'Pain and Heartache' in the Texas Senate During Debate on Confederate Monuments," *The Texas Tribune*, May 7, 2019; https://www .texastribune.org/2019/05/07/texas-confederate-monuments-harder-remove -under-senate-bill/.

25. Steven Pedigo, "Texas Metros Are Booming: The Guv and the Lege Keep Getting in Their Way," *Texas Monthly*, August 20, 2021; https://www .texasmonthly.com/news-politics/census-growth-diversity-metros/.

26. Alexa Ura and Emma Platoff, "Federal Judge Upholds Texas' Partisan Statewide Judicial Elections System," *The Texas Tribune,* September 12, 2018; https://www.texastribune.org/2018/09/12/statewide-judicial-elections-federal -judge-upholds-partisan/.

27. The model is described statistically in table A1 of the appendix. The dependent variable in the analysis, meaning the variable we are attempting to explain

is the five-point party identification scale. Our independent variables are demographic variables such as race/ethnicity (White, Latino, and Black, compared to "other;"), gender (male as opposed to female), and age (five-point scale); socioeconomic variables such as education (the revised five-category scale), and household income (revised five-point scale); political ideology; and religious variables such as religious identity (evangelical Protestant, Roman Catholic, mainline Protestant, African American Protestant, and secular, compared to "other religion;"); the importance of religion in your life (four-point scale); how often one attends worship services (five-category scale); and marital status (married as opposed to not married).

28. Erin Simon, "Texas Lieutenant Governor Falsely Claims That Unvaccinated Black Texans Are to Blame for COVID Surge," CNNWire, August 21, 2021; accessed: https://abc7.com/dan-patrick-texas-lt-governor-blames-black-people -unvaccinated/10966166/.

29. Robert S. Erikson, Gerald C. Wright, and John P. McIver, *Statehouse Democracy: Public Opinion and Policy in the American States* (New York: Cambridge University Press, 2013); Gerald Wright and Elizabeth Rigby, "Income Inequality and State Parties: Who Gets Represented?" *State Politics and Policy Quarterly* 20(4): 395–415.

30. As with the 2018 data, we also ran our regression analysis using only White respondents in 2020. Again, the results were nearly identical in every way for Whites only, the married variable was not a significant predictor of party identity in 2020. Some researchers have noted that because African Americans are so prone to identify with Democrats and even Latinos tend to be more pro-Democratic Party as a group than do Whites, that it is more likely that Whites are affected by variables other than race in terms of partisan attitudes and behavior. Here, we have found that Whites are no different than non-Whites, which adds to the robustness of the findings we have reported here and in appendix table A.1.

Chapter 3: Lone Star Split: Regional Political Identities

1. Paul Benson, David Clinkscale, and Anthony Giardino, *Lone Star Politics* (London: Pearson, 2011).

2. Julian Esparza, "Sen. John Cornyn Makes Campaign Stop in Tyler: The Senator Is on a Campaign Bus Tour Across the State," KLTV (Tyler, TX), October 29, 2020; https://www.kltv.com/2020/10/29/sen-john-cornyn-makes-campaign -stop-tyler/

3. Earl Black and Merle Black, *Politics and Society in the South* (Cambridge, MA:

Harvard University Press, 1987). Irwin Morris, *Movers and Stayers: The Partisan Transformation of 21st Century Southern Politics* (New York: Oxford University Press, 2021).

4. Zoe Nemerever and Melissa Rogers, "Measuring the Rural Continuum in Political Science," *Political Analysis* (2021): 1–20; https://doi.org/10.1017/pan .2020.47.

5. James Gimpel and Iris Hui, "Seeking Politically Compatible Neighbors? The Role of Neighborhood Partisan Composition in Residential Sorting," *Political Geography* 35, no. 1(2015): 1–13. Clayton Nall, *The Road to Inequality: How the Federal Highway Program Polarized America and Undermined Cities* (New York: Cambridge University Press, 2018). See also, Jonathan Mummolo and Clayton Nall, "Why Partisans Do Not Sort: The Constraints on Political Segregation," *Journal of Politics* 79, no. 1 (2017): 45–59.

6. Samara Klar, "Partisanship in a Social Setting," *American Journal of Political Science* 58, no. 3 (2014): 687–704.

7. Todd Gilman, "Jill Biden to Visit Texas as Early Voting Opens," *Dallas Morning News* 8B, October 10, 2020; https://www.dallasnews.com/news/politics /2020/10/09/joe-biden-sending-jill-biden-to-texas-as-dems-ramp-up-investment -in-long-neglected-state/.

8. Texas Department of Health and Human Services, 2020; https://www.dshs .state.tx.us/hivstd/reports/border/sec2.shtm.

9. In the 2020 election, voter turnout in El Paso County was 12 percent lower than the percent of registered voters across the state who voted. We omitted 2020 from this direct comparison because during the 2020 election, the El Paso County government mandated a stay-at-home order to combat the spread of the coronavirus.

10. Martin Waldron, "Chicanos in Texas Bid for Key Political Role," *New York Times*, 1A, August 2, 1970; https://www.nytimes.com/1970/08/02/archives /chicanos-in-texas-bid-for-key-political-role-chicanos-in-texas-in.html.

11. Christopher Giles, "Trump's Wall: How Much Has Been Built During His Term?" BBC, January 12, 2021; https://www.bbc.com/news/world-us -canada-46748492.

12. Liz Stark, "Trump Says He "Wouldn't Mind" Visiting Detention Facility While in Texas," CNN, January 10, 2019; https://www.cnn.com/politics/live-news /trump-border-visit-january-2019/index.html.

Chapter 4: The Reemergence of Texas Democrats on the National Stage

1. Beto O'Rourke, "Democratic Presidential Debate," *CNN* (Detroit, MI), June 26, 2019.

2. M. V. Hood, III and Set McKee, "What Made Carolina Blue? In-Migration and the 2008 North Carolina Presidential Vote," *American Politics Review* 38, no. 2 (2010): 266–302.

3. Karen L. Owen, "Georgia: Rebirth of Two-Party Competition" in *Presidential Swing States*, eds. David Schultz and Stacey Hunter Hecht (Lanham, MD: Rowman & Littlefield, 2021).

4. Gary C. Jacobson, *A Divider, Not a Uniter: George W. Bush and the American People.* (London: Longman, 2006).

5. Harold W. Stanley and Charles D. Hadley, "The Southern Presidential Primary: Regional Intentions with National Implications," *Publius: The Journal of Federalism* 17, no. 3 (1987): 83–100.

6. David Broder, "The Democrats' Dilemma: There Is Less to the Party's Prospects Than Meets the Eye," *The Atlantic Monthly* 233, no. 3 (1974): 31–40.

7. Former U.S. Representative John Delaney (D-MD) and Andrew Yang announced their candidacy in 2017.

8. James E. Campbell, *The American Campaign: U.S. Presidential Campaigns and the National Vote*, 2nd ed (College Station: Texas A&M University Press, 2008).

9. Campbell argues that *narrowing effects* operate at the same time as momentum, but the two are separate phenomena. Momentum can be gained in the short term as events unfold to the advantage of one candidate or the other, so a candidate can lose momentum as fast as it is earned.

10. Larry Bartels, *Presidential Primaries and the Dynamics of Public Choice* (Princeton, NJ: Princeton University Press, 1988).

11. Patrick J. Kenney and Tom W. Rice, "The Psychology of Political Momentum," *Political Research Quarterly* 47, no. 4 (1994): 923–38.

12. See Alex Samuels and Carla Astudillo, "Here's How the Top Democratic Presidential Candidates Are Faring in the Race for Texas Donors," *Texas Tribune* (Austin), October 18, 2019; https://www.texastribune.org/2019/10/18/texas-presidential-donations-heres-how-top-democrats-compare/.

13. Todd Gillman and Tom Benning, "Here's How the Texans, Biden, Warren, and Sanders Fared in Marathon Democratic Debate," *Dallas MorningNews*, September 12, 2019; https://www.dallasnews.com/news/politics/2019/09/12/here-s-how-the-texans-biden-warren-and-sanders-fared-in-marathon-democratic-debate/

Chapter 5: Primaries and WhataBiden! on Super Tuesday

1. Brian Sweany and Paul Burka, "What Happened to David Dewhurst?" *Texas Monthly*, June 2, 2014; https://www.texasmonthly.com/burka-blog/what-happened-to-david-dewhurst/.

2. Richard Boyd, "The Effects of Primaries and Statewide Races on Voter Turnout," *Journal of Politics* 51, no. 3 (1989): 730–39.

3. Jamie Lovegrove, "Jim Clyburn Gives Influential Endorsement to Joe Biden Days Before South Carolina's 2020 Primary," *Post and Courier* (Charleston, SC), February 26, 2020.

4. Sean McMinn, "How Many Delegates Do the 2020 Democratic Presidential Candidates Have?" *Texas Public Radio* (Austin, TX), March 11, 2020.

5. Matthew Barreto, *Ethnic Cues: The Role of Shared Ethnicity in Latino Political Participation* (Ann Arbor: University of Michigan Press, 2010). Gary C. Jacobson, *The Politics of Congressional Elections*, 2 ed. (Boston: Little Brown, 1987).

6. Editorial Board, "In the Democratic Primary for U.S. Senate, We Recommend Two Strong Contenders," *Dallas Morning News*, 2P, February 9, 2020.

7. Jonathan Tilove, "Senate Candidate 'Mamá' Garcia Isn't Hispanic But Says She Has 'el Corazón Latino,'" *Austin American-Statesman*, February 21, 2020.

8. Gromer Jeffers, "Senate Candidate Apologizes for Saying Her Surname, Tzintzún, Is 'More Mexican' Than Others," *Dallas Morning News* 1B, January 6, 2020.

9. Editorial Board, Interview with Senator John Cornyn, *Fort Worth Star-Telegram*, October 16, 2020.

10. Alan Abramowitz, John McGlennon, and Ronald Rapoport, "A Note on Strategic Voting in a Primary Election," *Journal of Politics* 43, no. 3 (1981): 899–904. D. Sunshine Hillygus and Sarah A. Truel, "Assessing Strategic Voting in the 2008 US Presidential Primaries: The Role of Electoral Context, Institutional Rules, and Negative Votes," *Public Choice* 161, no. 3 (2014): 517–36.

11. Keith T. Poole and Howard Rosenthal, *Congress: A Political-Economic History of Roll Call Voting* (New York: Oxford University Press, 1997).

Chapter 6: A Sleeping Giant: The Changing Electorate

1. Gromer Jeffers Jr., "After 2018 Warning Shot, Texas GOP Outworked State's Democrats to Keep State Red," *Dallas Morning News*, 1A, November 5, 2020.

2. Gromer Jeffers Jr., "Republicans Send Democrats and Election Day Message: Texas Is Still Red," *Dallas Morning News*, 1A, November 4, 2020.

3. Ibid.

4. Ibid.

5. Ibid.

6. Benjamin Marquez, *Democratizing Texas: Race, Identity, and Mexican American Empowerment, 1945–2002* (Austin: University of Texas Press, 2019).

7. Nicole Narea and Dylan Scott, "The Price—and Big Potential Payoff—of Turning Texas Blue," *Vox*, September 21, 2020; https://www.vox.com/policy-and -politics/21417460/texas-blue-democrat-biden-beto-2020-election.

8. Texas Labor Market Information, "Historical Unemployment Rates (Seasonally Adjusted," Texas Workforce Commission; https://texaslmi.com/; accessed October 8, 2021.

9. Patrick Svitek, "President Donald Trump to Visit Dallas as He Resumes In-Person Campaign Fundraisers," *Texas Tribune*, May 29, 2020; https://www .texastribune.org/2020/05/29/president-trump-visit-dallas-texas-campaign -fundraiser-coronavirus/.

10. David Jackson, "Donald Trump Plans to Travel to West Texas for Campaign Fundraiser Despite COVID Spike," *USA Today*, July 9, 2020; https://www .usatoday.com/story/news/politics/2020/07/09/despite-covid-donald-trump -heads-west-texas-raise-campaign-cash/5404385002/.

11. Anna Novak, Mitchell Ferman, and Mandi Cai, "How Coronavirus Impacted the Texas Economy," *Texas Tribune*, June 26, 2021; https://apps.texastribune.org /features/2020/texas-unemployment/; accessed October 8, 2021.

12. Todd J. Gilman, "Cornyn Alters Donald Trump Jr. Appeal, Says It's No Big Deal," *Dallas Morning News*, 6A, September 18, 2019.

13. Michael S. Lewis-Beck, William G. Jacoby, Helmut Norpoth, and Herbert F. Weisber, *The American Voter Revisited* (Ann Arbor: University of Michigan Press, 2008); Gerald M. Pomper, "The Presidential Election," in Gerald M. Pomper, Ross K. Baker, Kathleen A. Frankovic, Charles E. Jacob, Wilson Carey McWilliams, and Henry A. Plotkin, *The Election of 1980: Reports and Interpretations* (Chatham, NJ: Chatham House, 1981); Gerald M. Pomper, "The Presidential Election," in Gerald M. Pomper, Ross K. Baker, Charles E. Jacob, Scott Keeter, Wilson Carey McWilliams, and Henry A. Plotkin, *The Election of 1984: Reports and Interpretations* (Chatham, NJ: Chatham House, 1985).

14. The full model improved the accuracy of predicting a voter's choice for president by 24 percent over a 71 percent chance from a random choice. The model for the Senate election improved the accuracy by 31 percent over the expected 61 percent from a random draw. These results are found in table A.2 of the appendix.

15. Alan I. Abramowitz, *The Great Alignment: Race, Party Transformation, and the Rise of Donald Trump* (New Haven, CT: Yale University Press, 2018); Earl Black and Merle Black, *The Rise of Southern Republicans* (Cambridge, MA:

Harvard University Press, 2002); Gary C. Jacobson, *The Politics of Congressional Elections,* 8th ed. (Boston: Pearson, 2013); Lewis-Beck, et al., *The American Voter Revisited.*

16. James E. Campbell, *Cheap Seats: The Democratic Party's Advantage in U.S. House Elections* (Columbus: Ohio State University Press, 1996); Abramowitz, *The Disappearing Center* (New Haven: Yale University Press, 2010); Abramowitz, *The Great Alignment*; Aldrich, John H., Jamie L. Carson, Brad T. Gomez, and David W. Rohde., *Change and Continuity in the 2016 and 2018 Elections* (Thousand Oaks, CA: CQ Press, 2020). Lewis-Beck, et al., have noted that the American National Election Studies (ANES) identified small gender gaps as early as the 1950s, but in the opposite direction with women more likely to support Republicans. According to the ANES, the trend reversed to the current pattern in the 1960s and was solidified by the 1970s. See Lewis-Beck, et al., *The American Voter Revisited.*

17. Views on the border wall and DACA have a weak correlation (0.23%) across the 3,195 interviews when both questions were asked.

Chapter 7: Race and Social Justice in Texas Politics

1. Andy Rose, "Houston Police Chief: Defunding Law Enforcement Would Be 'An Invitation to Chaos,'" CNN, June 9, 2020.

2. Ian Haney López, *Dog Whistle Politics: How Coded Racial Appeals Have Reinvented Racism and Wrecked the Middle Class* (Oxford: Oxford University Press, 2003), 1.

3. Ibid., 2.

4. Ibid.

5. Rick Perlstein, "Exclusive: Lee Atwater's Infamous 1981 Interview on the Southern Strategy," *The Nation*, November 13, 2012; https://www.thenation.com /article/archive/exclusive-lee-atwaters-infamous-1981-interview-southern-strategy/.

6. In 1997, the Texas Senate tried to replace affirmative action that allowed state universities to grant access based on minority status to allowing state universities to grant automatic admission to high school graduates who finished in the top 10 percent of their class. This move was on the heels of *Hopewood v. Texas*—where a federal court decided that the University of Texas Law School's admissions policy violated the civil rights of four nonminority applicants using race as a criterion in granting admittance. *Hopwood v. Texas—Significance, Denied Admission, Millions in Damages, the Terms of the Complaint, the Former Policy* (1996). Law Library—American Law and Legal Information; https://law.jrank.org/pages /13111/Hopwood-v-Texas.html.

7. Sam Howe Verhovek highlights how resistance against housing integration in the 1990s in Vidor, Texas, prompted federal intervention; see Verhovek, "Blacks Moved to Texas Housing Project," *The New York Times*, January 14, 1994, sec. U.S.; https://www.nytimes.com/1994/01/14/us/blacks-moved-to-texas-housing-project.html.

8. According to Soss, et al.,: "In the period immediately following federal legislation in 1996, the strictest welfare reforms were significantly more likely to be adopted in states where people of color made up a larger proportion of welfare caseload. Public support for these tough new welfare measures arose from many sources. But support ran stronger among whites than Blacks, and within the white population support was significantly enhanced by stereotypes of African Americans and Hispanics." Texas reformed (and reduced) its welfare rolls in 1996. O'Brien, Erin, *Race and the Politics of Welfare Reform*, eds., Joe Soss, Sanford F. Schram, and Thomas P. Vartania (Ann Arbor: University of Michigan Press, 2003), 226.

9. Texas Governor William Clements, the first Republican governor since Reconstruction, openly ceded "the drug issue" to the federal government. At that time, the Reagan administration's "anti-drug rhetoric was skillfully designed to tap into deeply held cultural attitudes about people of color and their links to drug use and other illicit behavior." According to scholar William Elwood, "Reagan's rhetorical declaration of a war on drugs had a deliberate political effect. Such rhetoric allows presidents to appear as strong leaders who are tough on crime and concerned about domestic issues and is strategically ambiguous to portray urban minorities as responsible for problems related to the drug war and for resolving such problems." Kenneth B. Nunn, "Race, Crime and the Pool of Surplus Criminality: Or Why the 'War on Drugs' Was a 'War on Blacks,'" *Gender, Race, and Justice* 6 (2002): 381–445, 386–412, 422–27.

10. Robert C. Smith, *We Have No Leaders: African Americans in the Post-Civil Rights Era* (Albany: State University of New York Press).

11. Steven Hoenisch, "Crime Policy of the Republican Party," in *The Encyclopedia of the American Democratic and Republican Parties*, International Encyclopedia Society, 2004; https://www.criticism.com/policy/republicans-crime-policy.php.

12. John R. Petrocik, "Issue Ownership in Presidential Elections, with a 1980 Case Study," *American Journal of Political Science* 40 no. 3 (1996): 825–50. Also, John R. Petrocik, William L. Benoit, and Glenn J. Hansen, "Issue Ownership and Presidential Campaigning, 1952–2000," *Political Science Quarterly* 118 no. 4 (2003): 599–626.

13. LeAnn M. Brazeal and William L. Benoit, "Issue Ownership in Congressional Campaign Television Spots," *Communication Quarterly* 56 no. 1 (2018): 17–28.

14. Juliana M. Horowitz and Gretchen Livingston, "How Americans View the

Black Lives Matter Movement," Pew Research Center, July 8, 2016; https://www
.pewresearch.org/fact-tank/2016/07/08/how-americans-view-the-black-lives
-matter-movement/.

15. Kenneth Bryant Jr., "Black and Blue: Exploring Protests, African American Attitudes, and Law Enforcement Behavior" (Typescript: University of Missouri, 2017).

16. Jules Witcover, *The Year the Dream Died: Revisiting 1968 in America* (New
York: Warner Books, 1997).

17. Juan Pablo Garnham, "In Fort Worth, Activists Are Hoping Voters Will Re-
duce the Local Police Budget by as Much as $80 Million," *The Eagle*, July 14, 2020;
https://theeagle.com/news/state-and-regional/in-fort-worth-activists-are-hoping
-voters-will-reduce-the-local-police-budget-by-as/article_388ba667-d4eb-5ed5
-acb5-2de666581e62.html.

18. Robert T. Garrett, "Abbott Pushing Legislation to Strip Cities of Local Sales
Tax Funds If They 'Defund the Police,'" *The Dallas Morning News*, January 14,
2021; https://www.dallasnews.com/news/politics/2021/01/15/abbott-considers
-bill-to-strip-cities-of-local-sales-tax-funds-if-they-defund-the-police/.

19. Jack Citrin, Donald Philip Green, and David O. Sears, "White Reactions
to Black Candidates: When Does Race Matter?" *Public Opinion Quarterly* 54, no.
1(1988): 74-96 .

20. Ibid., 2.

21. Victor D. Hanson, "Illegal Immigration Ideology: Orwellian, Virtue-
Signaling," *National Review*, April 10, 2018; https://www.nationalreview.com/2018
/04/illegal-immigration-ideology-orwellian-virtue-signaling/.

22. Caitlin McFall, "Montana Bans Sanctuary Cities for Illegal Immigrants," Fox
News, April 3, 2021; https://www.foxnews.com/politics/montana-bans-sanctuary
-cities-for-illegal-immigrants.

23. Anthony W. Fontes, "Republican Ads Feature MS-13, Hoping Fear Will Motivate Voters," *The Conversation*, November 2, 2018; http://theconversation.com
/republican-ads-feature-ms-13-hoping-fear-will-motivate-voters-105474.

24. Lila Valencia, "Texas Demographic Trends and the Upcoming 2020 Census,"
Texas Demographic Center, March 4, 2020; https://demographics.texas.gov
/Resources/Presentations/OSD/2020/2020_03_04_MetropolitanBreakfastClub
.pdf.

Chapter 8: Selective Media Exposure and Political Attitudes

1. Matthew McConaughey, "Actor and Author Matthew McConaughey Speaks
with CNBC's Carl Quintanilla Live During CNBC's @Work Summit Today,"
CNBC, March 30, 2021.

2. Cass R. Sunstein, *Going to Extremes: How Like Minds Unite and Divide* (Oxford University Press, 2009).

3. Dave Richards, "Lifestyles of the Rich and Infamous," *Texas Observer*, November 28, 2008; https://www.texasobserver.org/2913-lifestyles-of-the-rich-and-infamous/.

4. Solomon Messing, Patrick van Kessel, and Adam Hughes, "Sharing the News in a Polarized Congress," *Pew Research Center* (blog), December 18, 2017; https://www.pewresearch.org/politics/2017/12/18/sharing-the-news-in-a-polarized-congress/.

5. James Druckman, Erik Petersen, and Rune Slothuus, "How Elite Polarization Affects Public Opinion Formation," *American Political Science Review* 107(1): 57–79.

6. Matthew S. Levendusky, "Why Do Partisan Media Polarize Viewers?" *American Journal of Political Science* 57 no. 3 (2013): 611–23; Silvia Knobloch-Westerwick and Jingbo Meng, "Looking the Other Way: Selective Exposure to Attitude-Consistent and Counterattitudinal Political Information," *Communication Research* 36 no. 3 (2009): 426–48; R. Kelly Garrett, "Politically Motivated Reinforcement Seeking: Reframing the Selective Exposure Debate," *Journal of Communication* 59 no. 4 (2009): 676–99; https://doi.org/10.1111/j.1460-2466.2009.01452.x.

7. Diana C. Mutz, *Hearing the Other Side: Deliberative Versus Participatory Democracy* (Cambridge: Cambridge University Press, 2006); Eric Lawrence, John Sides, and Henry Farrell, "Self-Segregation or Deliberation? Blog Readership, Participation, and Polarization in American Politics," *Perspectives on Politics* 8 no. 1 (2010): 141–57; Shanto Iyengar and Sean J. Westwood, "Fear and Loathing across Party Lines: New Evidence on Group Polarization," *American Journal of Political Science* 59 no. 3 (2015): 690–707; https://doi.org/10.1111/ajps.12152.

8. Shanto Iyengar, Gaurav Sood, and Yphtach Lelkes, "Affect, Not Ideology: A Social Identity Perspective on Polarization," *Public Opinion Quarterly* 76 no. 3 (2012): 405–31; https://doi.org/10.1093/poq/nfs038.

9. Natalie Jomini Stroud, *Niche News: The Politics of News Choice* (New York: Oxford University Press, 2011); R. Kelly Garrett and Natalie Jomini Stroud, "Partisan Paths to Exposure Diversity: Differences in Pro- and Counterattitudinal News Consumption," *Journal of Communication* 64 no. 4 (2014): 680–701; https://doi.org/10.1111/jcom.12105; Shanto Iyengar and Kyu S. Hahn, "Red Media, Blue Media: Evidence of Ideological Selectivity in Media Use," *Journal of Communication* 59 no. 1 (2009): 19–39; https://doi.org/10.1111/j.1460-2466.2008.01402.x.

10. Mark Jurkowitz, Amy Mitchell, Elisa Shearer, and Mason Walker, "U.S. Media Polarization and the 2020 Election: A Nation Divided," *Pew Research*

Center's Journalism Project (blog), January 24, 2020; https://www.journalism
.org/2020/01/24/u-s-media-polarization-and-the-2020-election-a-nation-divided/.

11. Natalie Jomini Stroud, "Polarization and Partisan Selective Exposure," *Journal of Communication* 60 no. 3 (2010): 556–76; https://doi.org/10.1111/j.1460
-2466.2010.01497.x; Mutz, *Hearing the Other Side.*

12. Levendusky, "Why Do Partisan Media Polarize Viewers?"; Matthew A.
Baum and Tim Groeling, "Reality Asserts Itself: Public Opinion on Iraq and the
Elasticity of Reality," *International Organization* 64 no. 3 (2010): 443–79; Kathleen Hall Jamieson and Joseph N. Cappella, *Echo Chamber: Rush Limbaugh and
the Conservative Media Establishment* (New York: Oxford University Press, 2008).

13. Sunstein, *Going to Extremes.*

14. Kevin Arceneaux, Martin Johnson, and John Cryderman, "Communication,
Persuasion, and the Conditioning Value of Selective Exposure: Like Minds May
Unite and Divide but They Mostly Tune Out," *Political Communication* 30 no. 2
(2013): 213–31; https://doi.org/10.1080/10584609.2012.737424.

15. Robert Huckfeldt, Paul E. Johnson, and John Sprague, *Political Disagreement: The Survival of Diverse Opinions Within Communication Networks.* (Cambridge: Cambridge University Press, 2004).

16. Mutz, *Hearing the Other Side*, 2.

17. Diana C. Mutz, "Cross-Cutting Social Networks: Testing Democratic Theory in Practice," *American Political Science Review* 96 no. 1 (2002): 111–26; https://
doi.org/10.1017/S0003055402004264.

18. Mutz, *Hearing the Other Side.*

19. Ibid.

20. Huckfeldt, Johnson, and Sprague, *Political Disagreement.*

21. Levendusky, "Why Do Partisan Media Polarize Viewers?"

22. Natalie Jomini Stroud, *Niche News: The Politics of News Choice* (New York:
Oxford University Press, 2011); R. Lance Holbert, R. Kelly Garrett, and Laurel S.
Gleason, "A New Era of Minimal Effects? A Response to Bennett and Iyengar,"
Journal of Communication 60 no. 1 (2010): 15–34; https://doi.org/10.1111/j
.1460-2466.2009.01470.x.

23. Stroud, "Polarization and Partisan Selective Exposure."

24. Levendusky, "Why Do Partisan Media Polarize Viewers?"

25. Gangheong Lee and Joseph N. Cappella, "The Effects of Political Talk Radio
on Political Attitude Formation: Exposure Versus Knowledge," *Political Communication* 18(4): 369–94.

26. John R. Zaller, *The Nature and Origins of Mass Partisanship* (Cambridge:
Cambridge: Cambridge University Press, 1992).

27. Dolores Albarracín and Amy L. Mitchell, "The Role of Defensive Confi-

dence in Preference for Proattitudinal Information: How Believing That One Is Strong Can Sometimes Be a Defensive Weakness," *Personality & Social Psychology Bulletin* 30 no. 12 (2004): 1565–84; https://doi.org/10.1177/0146167204271180.

28. A few things about our methodology: We asked survey respondents questions about which TV and radio programs they watched or listened to on a regular basis (and their social media sources). If they selected a "liberal" network such as MSNBC, we define that as the respondent using partisan liberal media. If they selected a conservative network such as Fox News, we define that as using partisan conservative media. We operationalize cross-cutters as respondents who indicate they are Democrats or Republicans but use partisan media from their side, as well as the other side of the political spectrum. Odd-partisans are Democrats or Republicans who use partisan media from the other side, but not partisan media that agrees with them. Hyperpartisans are Democrats or Republicans who use partisan media that agrees with their stated party identification.

29. Brandon Mulder, "Alex Jones Leads Anti-Mask Protest at Capitol," *Austin American-Statesman*, June 28, 2020; https://www.statesman.com/story/news/local/2020/06/28/alex-jones-leads-anti-mask-protest-at-capitol/113734628/.

30. Kathleen Hall Jamieson and Dolores Albarracín, "The Relation between Media Consumption and Misinformation at the Outset of the SARS-CoV-2 Pandemic in the US," *Harvard Kennedy School Misinformation Review* 1, April 2020; https://doi.org/10.37016/mr-2020-012, 1.

31. Rasha Ali, "Trish Regan, Fox Business Parts Ways Shortly after Her Coronavirus 'Impeachment Scam' Comments," *USA TODAY*, March 28, 2020; https://www.usatoday.com/story/entertainment/celebrities/2020/03/28/fox-business-parts-ways-trish-regan-after-coronavirus-comments/2932616001/.

32. Ceren Budak, Ashley Muddiman, and Natalie (Talia) Stroud, "How Did U.S. Television News Networks Cover the Pandemic? Here's a Scorecard," *Washington Post*, February 3, 2021; https://www.washingtonpost.com/politics/2021/02/03/how-did-different-us-television-news-networks-cover-pandemic-heres-scorecard/.

33. Ibid.

34. Ibid.

35. Tucker Carlson, "The Real Reason Mobs across the Country Are Tearing Down American Monuments," Fox News, June 23, 2020; https://www.foxnews.com/opinion/tucker-carlson-the-real-reason-mobs-across-the-country-are-tearing-down-american-monuments.

36. Courtney Hagle, "Right-Wing Media Vilify Black Lives Matter as the Movement Grows," Media Matters for America, June 24, 2020; https://www.mediamatters.org/black-lives-matter/right-wing-media-vilify-black-lives-matter-movement-grows.

37. Bryan D. Wright, "NFL Protests: Stars Should Get off Their Knees and Lead a Constructive Conversation on Race," Fox News, September 26, 2017; https://www.foxnews.com/opinion/nfl-protests-stars-should-get-off-their-knees-and-lead-a-constructive-conversation-on-race.

38. Benjamin Sachs and Noah Zatz, "The Law Is on the NFL Players' Side," *New York Times*, October 17, 2017, sec. Opinion; https://www.nytimes.com/2017/10/17/opinion/law-nfl-protests.html.

39. Elizabeth Greico, "Americans' Main Sources for Political News Vary by Party and Age," *Pew Research Center* (blog), April 1, 2020; https://www.pewresearch.org/fact-tank/2020/04/01/americans-main-sources-for-political-news-vary-by-party-and-age/.

40. John Sands, "Local News Is More Trusted than National News—but That Could Change," Knight Foundation, October 29, 2019; https://knightfoundation.org/articles/local-news-is-more-trusted-than-national-news-but-that-could-change/.

41. Ibid.

42. Clara Hendrickson, "Local Journalism in Crisis: Why America Must Revive Its Local Newsrooms," *Brookings* (blog), November 12, 2019; https://www.brookings.edu/research/local-journalism-in-crisis-why-america-must-revive-its-local-newsrooms/.

43. Ibid.

44. Ibid.

45. Tom Stites, "A Quarter of All U.S. Newspapers Have Died in 15 Years, a New UNC News Deserts Study Found," *Poynter* (blog), June 24, 2020; https://www.poynter.org/locally/2020/unc-news-deserts-report-2020/.

46. Andrea Guzmán, "No News Is Bad News," *Texas Observer*, February 11, 2019; https://www.texasobserver.org/no-news-is-bad-news/.

47. Ibid.; Joshua P. Darr, Matthew P. Hitt, and Johanna L Dunaway, "Newspaper Closures Polarize Voting Behavior," *Journal of Communication* 68 no. 6 (2008): 1007–28; https://doi.org/10.1093/joc/jqy051.

48. Twitter, "Permanent Suspension of @realDonaldTrump," January 8, 2021; https://blog.twitter.com/en_us/topics/company/2020/suspension.html.

49. Mark Zuckerberg, "Banning Donald Trump from Facebook," Facebook, January 7, 2021; https://www.facebook.com/zuck/posts/10112681480907401.

50. Emily A. Vogels, Andrew Perrin, and Monica Anderson, "Most Americans Think Social Media Sites Censor Political Viewpoints," *Pew Research Center: Internet, Science & Tech* (blog), August 19, 2020; https://www.pewresearch.org/internet/2020/08/19/most-americans-think-social-media-sites-censor-political-viewpoints/.

51. Brittany Berstein, "Donald Trump to Launch Platform, Adviser Says," *National Review*, March 22, 2021; https://www.nationalreview.com/news/trump -to-launch-social-media-platform-adviser-says/.

52. Alex Thompson, "Why the Right Wing Has a Massive Advantage on Facebook," *POLITICO*, September 26, 2020; https://www.politico.com/news/2020 /09/26/facebook-conservatives-2020-421146.

53. Paul M. Barrett and J. Grant Sims, "False Accusation: The Unfounded Claim That Social Media Companies Censor Conservatives," *NYU Center for Business and Human Rights*, February 2021; https://static1.squarespace.com/static /5b6df958f8370af3217d4178/t/60187b5f45762e708708c8e9/1612217185240 /NYU+False+Accusation_2.pdf.

54. Cameron Langford, "Texas Republicans Take on Social Media Titans in 'Deplatforming' Bill," *Courthouse News Service* (blog), March 9, 2021; https://www .courthousenews.com/texas-republicans-take-on-social-media-titans-in -deplatforming-bill/.

55. Brandon Doyle, "TikTok Statistics–Everything You Need to Know," *Wallaroo Media* (blog), February 6, 2021; https://wallaroomedia.com/blog/social -media/tiktok-statistics/.

56. Katie Sehl, "Instagram Demographics in 2021: Important User Stats for Marketers," *Social Media Marketing & Management Dashboard* (blog), January 27, 2021; https://blog.hootsuite.com/instagram-demographics/.

57. Barrett and Sims, "False Accusation."

58. Adept Plus, "Nielsen DMA Rankings 2020," MediaTracks Communications; https://mediatracks.com/resources/nielsen-dma-rankings-2020/.

59. Alex Samuels, "Hey, Texplainer: How Much Does It Cost to Run for Office in Texas?" *Texas Tribune*, November 10, 2017; https://www.texastribune.org /2017/11/10/hey-texplainer-how-much-does-it-cost-run-office-texas/.

Chapter 9: Texas's New Two-Party Dance

1. V. O. Key Jr., *Southern Politics in State and Nation* (New York: Knopf, 1949).

2. Jonathan Tilove, "Royce West Won't Vote for M. J. Hegar: 'She's Had a Problem All Along with Black Folks,'" *Austin-American Statesman*, October 9, 2020; https://www.statesman.com/story/news/politics/government/2020/10/10/royce -west-wonrsquot-vote-for-mj-hegar-shersquos-had-problem-all-along-with-black -folksrsquo/114253566/.

3. Huerta, Carlos and Beatriz Cuartas. 2021. "Red to Purple? Changing Demographics and Party Change in Texas." *Social Science Quarterly* 102(4): 1330-1348

4. Peter Enns and Julianna Koch, "Public Opinion in the U.S. States: 1956 to 2010." *State Politics & Policy Quarterly* 13(3): 429–372.

5. Jeronimo Cortina, "From a Distance: Geographic Proximity, Partisanship, and Public Attitudes toward the U.S.-Mexico Border Wall," *Political Research Quarterly* 73 no. 3 (2020): 740–54.

6. Julian Aguilar, "As Government Prepares to Seize More Land for a Border Wall, Some Texas Landowners Prepare to Fight," *Texas Tribune*, November 21, 2019; https://www.texastribune.org/2019/11/21/texans-fight-government-plan-seize-land-border-wall/. Rachel Zohn, "Recent ICE Raids Overload Mississippi Legal System," *US News & World Report*, October 18, 2019; https://www.usnews.com/news/best-states/articles/2019-10-18/recent-ice-raids-by-us-immigration-and-customs-enforcement-overload-mississippi-legal-system.